C[illegible] on the Run

Gloria Guenther

Cat on the Run

Gloria Guenther

Windflower Communications
WINNIPEG, MANITOBA

Published by Windflower Communications,
#7-1110 Henderson Highway, Winnipeg, MB R2G 1L1

Special acknowledgement is made to the Toronto Humane Society for its most helpful assistance with research, and to the Toronto Sun for permission to quote from "Stubby Takes on the Rat Patrol" (January 15, 1985).

Canadian Cataloguing in Publication Data
Guenther, Gloria
Cat on the run

ISBN 1-895308-00-3

I. Title.

PS8563.U297C3 1991 jC813/ .54 C91-097132-3
PZ10.3.G846Ca 1991

Cover and Illustrations by Gloria Guenther
Design by Publishing Services, Winnipeg, MB
Printed in the United States by Evangel Press, Nappanee, IN

International Standard Book Number: 1-895308-00-3

LOVINGLY DEDICATED
TO MY HUSBAND
who agrees
that four cats are NOT too many

Chapter One

"Mother," I whined fretfully, "why must I be trapped forever inside this house? I want to explore the world and meet other cats."

Mother blinked her vivid blue eyes in amusement and tilted her ears toward me. "You're much too young, son. You would surely get lost or stolen. Besides, if the dogs and raccoons don't get you, Nasty Joe will. He's the terror of the entire Rosedale cat community! He rounds up stray cats and takes them out of town to a garbage dump for target practice."

I was so shocked I could hardly speak. "But why?" I gasped.

"He's a cat-hater! He does it to spite the strays who get into his garbage and keep him awake at night with their yowling. He's angry because they lie in his garden and wreck his beautiful flowers and chase the birds from his bird feeder."

I hissed angrily. "That's no excuse. He should be thrown in jail. He must be stopped!"

"I agree," Mother replied, "but there's nothing those helpless cats can do. You are much better off being an indoor cat. Besides, your father and I find competitive cat showing very exciting. I'm sure you will too. You'll travel and meet all sorts of famous Siamese showcats. You may even end up like your father in a major movie or nationally televised cat food commercial. So let's not hear any more nonsense about running away."

Mother stood up on the living room carpet and stretched luxuriously, kneading her claws in the rug as she leaned back in a deep, graceful bow. I glanced at the finely engraved name tag on Mother's jeweled collar, wishing for one of my own. The golden sunlight streamed through the window, gleaming on her satiny cream-colored fur. She sat down and yawned widely as I admired her smooth elegant form.

I caught a faint whiff of fish odor as I stared curiously into her gaping jaws. To me everything about Mother was beautiful, even the pink-ridged mouth with its impressive fangs and many small, needle-sharp teeth. She finished yawning and blinked her sapphire blue eyes, twining her long tapered tail around her body and tucking the end over her delicate paws. She sat poised like a regal queen, purring as she looked down at me.

As she began cleaning my fur, I purred contentedly. For the moment there was no more talk of running away. I thought instead of what it would be like to travel the show circuit like my famous parents. Perhaps, like Father, I too would experience the glamor and thrill of a film and modeling career. I yawned and curled up by Mother's side to purr myself to sleep.

Our home with Frank and Lorna Penner was in Rosedale, an exclusive part of Toronto. Their family room had one wall entirely covered with my parents' photographs, ribbons and awards. A large trophy case contained Father's C.F.A. Grand Champion certificate and rosette. We five kittens rarely saw our father since his career as a showcat involved constant travel.

One afternoon, my little sister watched sedately as Mother groomed me. Her satiny ears perked forward as she gazed into Mother's face and asked, "Mummy, I don't want to move away. Can't we all stay here together for always?"

"Are you kidding?" said one of our brothers. "I can hardly wait to get out and see the world."

Mother explained with a sigh, "I don't think any of you will end up in a home where you are not properly cared for or loved, but there are many homeless cats on the streets of Toronto. Poor, pathetic little scavengers; they feed from garbage-strewn alleyways, constantly stealing and fighting one another and other animals for a few scraps of food."

"But Mother," asked one of my brothers, "is there no one at all to care for them? Is there no place for them to go?"

Mother gazed sadly into his earnest little face and replied, "Oh yes, but there are still thousands of homeless strays – thousands. And many of the strays in animal shelters are in such poor health that they must be . . . but no, it is too sad. I can't bear to think of it!"

For once we did not squirm and frolic as she groomed each of us in turn. We snuggled close, confident that we need never worry about starvation or neglect – or Nasty Joe! Those terrible things happened to outsiders, the common domestics. Or so I thought!

In a few weeks I was the last kitten remaining at home. Mother reassured me that my brothers and sister had gone to good homes, but I could see that she missed them. Sometimes she paced the room as though searching for them and one afternoon she admitted that it was never easy for her to give up her children. "But it's for the best," she confided as we lay curled on a sunny window ledge.

She sighed and sat up to preen her long, slender body as she explained, "Your father and I have seen a number of our children take first place in a cat show. I'm sure that's why Penners have decided to keep you. You have unusual showcat potential, son."

That night as I settled down to sleep, I tried to picture all the fame and recognition that would be mine. Perhaps I would become a TV or movie star – and end up being even more famous than my father!

Several weeks passed by as I explored every room, closet, cupboard and piece of furniture in the house. I spent hours on the kitchen and living room window sills, sleeping in the sun or watching the activity outside. It seemed such an exciting place; I longed to go out and explore, but Mother reminded me I probably would be an "indoor cat" all my life as she had been.

I complained irritably, "That's not fair. I see all sorts of cats out there. Why can't I be out exploring and meeting other cats?"

"Yes, yes," she explained, "there are many domestic cats roaming the neighborhood, but you don't often see pedigreed showcats on the streets, and I don't wonder why. A torn ear or slash across the face could ruin your career – and those unpedigreed commoners are constantly squabbling!"

Mother looked me sternly in the eye as she continued to explain. "I managed to sneak out once, wanting to explore just like you, but I got lost and wandered all the way over to the Rosedale subway on Yonge Street. Some strays told me that many cats die in winter or get caught by Animal Control and are never heard of again. And of course there's the constant danger of Nasty Joe, not to mention the dogs, raccoons and poison traps. And vicious strays that will kill for a scrap of meat!

"Fortunately, some honest person turned me in. Poor Mrs. Penner thought I had been killed or stolen. I came home with a dreadful case of fleas!"

"Fleas?" I echoed.

"Yes – fleas!" she exclaimed. "Those vile insects drive you half-mad with the itching caused by their constant biting. It's so-o-o humiliating. You get hauled off to the vet for a flea bath."

"Why is it so humiliating?" I asked, trying not to laugh.

"They treat you like low-class scum, that's why," she replied haughtily. "The vet insinuated I'd caught them from keeping 'bad company.' The nerve!"

"But what did the vet do to you?" I asked.

"Well! Ask me what I did to the vet! I nearly tore the place apart. They tried to bathe me in a foul-smelling solution. I fought and hissed and scratched until someone jabbed me with a needle. I lost consciousness. When I woke up I was dizzy, and sick and damp from that revolting chemical. And my fur stank for days!"

I simply could not contain my laughter any longer and Mother swatted playfully at my head with a velvety paw. I tried to bat her back, but lost my balance and toppled over on the carpet.

One fall day as I gazed longingly from my place by the window, Mother joined me, landing in a feather-light leap on the ledge beside me. Outside autumn was especially tantalizing as brightly-hued leaves twirled and danced in the gusting wind and swirled across the lawns and walks. Sometimes my body jerked instinctively as leaves flew by the window and I would swipe eagerly at them, batting my paw uselessly at the windowpane. How I longed to be a part of that colorful, exciting scene.

Mother cleaned her fur, then settled down with paws tucked beneath her body. I began to plead, "Mother, I really would like to spend an afternoon exploring the neighborhood. Just once wouldn't hurt, would it? I long for adventure and excitement."

"Be patient, son. Believe me, competitive cat showing is most exciting. You have to expect to make some sacrifices."

"But what if all this stuff never happens? What if I don't even win the local competition? What then? I'll be stuck in this house for nothing – probably for the rest of my life."

"Even so," she replied, "it's not a bad life. You could so easily get lost or be stolen on the streets. You really must stop this nonsense talk of running away."

I thought peevishly, Mother worries needlessly. One of these days I'll slip out when no one's looking and just have a little snoop around. I could sneak off, enjoy a delightful outing and return safely home, before anyone noticed. What possible harm could that do?

Chapter Two

I thought my chance to escape would never come. The Penners were very watchful. Doors or windows were rarely left open in the winter. Even if I had managed to escape I would have soon returned, yowling to be let in from the cold.

One warm day in early spring, I was sitting with my nose pressed to the kitchen screen door. I often sat there, enjoying the new outdoor scents and sounds, longing to get out and explore. On this particular day I was irritable because some of the Penners' relatives had come to stay for a week. I especially disliked the boy and girl who constantly chased me around the house and tried to stuff me under their bedcovers at night. I spent much of my time hiding from the children.

Suddenly the two youngsters burst into the kitchen laughing and shouting in a game of tag. I shuffled away from the door and crouched along the wall as they yanked open the screen door and ran yelling and whooping into the backyard. For a split second the screen door hung wide open. I darted across the porch and under the hedges so quickly the children were not even aware I had escaped. In a few moments they were out of the yard and I was alone.

I remained crouched beneath the shrubs, trembling with nerves and excitement. It would be hours before anyone missed me since I had been in hiding for hours at a time.

The children returned and I backed up through the hedge, turned around and dashed across the neighbor's yard. I paused a moment, then ran down a small fence-bordered walkway and darted through the open gate into a back lane. I trotted along the dusty lane until the children's voices grew faint. I sniffed at plants and insects, pounced after butterflies and insects, and leaped at plants and grass that stirred in the breeze. At one point I flung myself over on my back, twisting and flipping about in the dust in an ecstasy of delight. Then I went to the side of the road and began nibbling on some tall grass. This upset my stomach, so I quit chewing at the blades and stems.

After an hour or so of wandering from one street to the next, I decided it was time to return home. I had been careful to avoid people and traffic. I stayed mostly in backyards and side lanes, running off whenever I saw other cats or heard dogs barking.

Suddenly, less than ten meters from where I stood, a screen door opened and a large dog came bounding out of the house and down the walk. He stopped dead the instant he saw me.

My back arched, fur bristled all over my body and my angry growl exploded into a long, furious hiss. I twisted sideways, arched tall and stiff-legged, staring the dog down and warning him off with a low, wailing growl. He lowered his head, bearing monstrous fangs in an evil snarl. I took off running for my life, ears and whiskers flat against my head!

The dog followed barking and yelping in mad excitement as I sped past a blur of yards, fences, shrubs, trees and swerving bicycles. I tried to lose him by leaping fences and scrambling under shrubs, but he remained on my trail, barking the whole time.

Suddenly a small fox terrier appeared, yapping and snarling. Their barking attracted other dogs that came leaping over fences, darting out of side streets, garages and back yards. Now I was really in trouble. It seemed when I lost one of my pursuers, another appeared out of nowhere.

I tore across the road, saw another dog headed straight at me and dashed back onto the road, right into the path of an oncoming car. The squeal of tires, blaring horn, yelping dogs and a wild, spinning sensation all seemed to happen at once. The world reeled crazily as I fought to regain consciousness. I lay half senseless on the ground, gasping for breath. Then I became aware of someone shouting. I tried to run, staggered dizzily and fell repeatedly, but somehow managed to make it off the street into a backyard.

Finally I did what I should have done the first moment I set eyes on that dog – I scrambled up a tree.

Panting heavily I crouched in the tree, hidden in the thick foliage, wishing with all my heart that I had never set foot out the door.

I dozed fitfully during the night, often startled awake by sudden or strange noises and mysterious rustling in the darkness. My whole body ached. I shivered in the cool dawn and began moving around to limber up my stiffened joints. Oh, how I longed for the sun-bathed warmth of my favorite window sill. I longed for my favorite tuna-flavored canned meat and creamy milk as well.

I sat on a branch, cleaning myself in preparation for the day. I edged my way carefully down onto the ground. I sniffed around, then sat, looking worriedly about. How would I ever find my way back? I had sped for miles without scenting or noticing anything around me. Oh well, I thought, perhaps some kind person will help me find my home. Then I remembered how Mother had spoken about her fear of being stolen. I also recalled the tales she had told about Nasty Joe and how he executed stray cats in the garbage dump. I shivered again!

I decided to wander for a while, trying to pick up a familiar scent or landmark but realized after an hour or so that I was completely and hopelessly lost!

During the lunch hour, I sniffed the delicious cooking odors that wafted in the air and wondered how to go about finding a meal. The thought of raiding garbage cans made me shudder, but I was willing to try it as a last resort. I had never killed a mouse in my life although I had caught and eaten the occasional fly and spider.

Someone turned on a water sprinkler and I crept around trying to find a way to get at the water. Eventually a few little rivulets formed along the sidewalk cracks. I lapped patiently until my thirst was quenched. I continued to wander aimlessly for several hours when I realized the traffic was far noisier. I also noticed a park close to a large, busy street with crowds of people hurrying along the wide sidewalks.

I observed several cats in the park and headed in their direction. One shabby gray had a torn ear and another smaller gray cat was missing chunks of fur around her neck. An orange tom turned his big head to stare at me, amber eyes narrowed suspiciously. The ill-tempered snarl on his battle-scarred face reminded me of the stories I'd heard about strays that would kill for a scrap of meat! A lean black cat sat grooming herself on a park bench. Her green eyes flashed a warning as our eyes met but she remained still, fur bristling slightly as I crept nearer.

I nearly lost my courage when a black and white cat caught sight of me and began ambling in my direction. I sat on the grass waiting for him to approach me. I waited tensely for his back to arch, expecting him to fly at me in a fur-bristling, spitting, snarling fit of fury! On the contrary, he walked up mildly and sat down a few meters away. He licked at his paw and I could smell a chicken-like fragrance as he began grooming himself.

He was a slender, wily-looking fellow, mostly black with some white patches. He seemed to have an awareness of everything that went on around him as he glanced here and there stealthily. When he stared at me with his large golden eyes, I felt as though he knew exactly what I was thinking. He gazed unwaveringly at me for several moments and then spoke. "You're new around this area, aren't you? Been gone from home long?"

"Uh – well actually, I'm lost. I've been lost since yesterday noon."

"Yeah?" He tilted his head and smiled shrewdly. "Well, you won't be homeless for long. If your owners don't find you, some cat-lover will carry you off. Folks pay big bucks for Siamese."

"Oh" was all I could answer.

He groomed busily for a few more seconds, then looked at me again with a curious expression and asked, "How ya makin' out on your own?"

"Well, actually – not too good. I'm half-starved."

"Too proud for the garbage bins, eh? You tried beggin' door-to-door? Fancy cat like you shouldn't have any problems. You'd be adopted in no time, I betcha. Just bat those baby blues and meow pretty!"

"I – I don't want to be stolen. I want to go back home. With my luck I'd end up in a home with half a dozen pesky kids."

"Well, you got a point there. Mind you, there's some mighty nasty adults too. One o' my best buddies was killed off by a guy called Nasty Joe!"

If Siamese could turn pale, I would have at that moment. I asked anxiously, "How do you know?"

"Know what?"

"That he – he kills them at the garbage dump."

"Don't be dumb! Some o' the strays find their way back and they tell us what goes on. Just the other night we had a meeting with one o' them, back of Harry's Diner. Let me tell you, kid, the Humane Society would have his hide if they knew what was going on. By the way, what's your name?"

"Shalom."

"Mine's Subway Pete. Got the name from hanging around the tracks. Which reminds me, we oughta see about getting you a bite to eat. Follow me."

Chapter Three

I followed obediently, expecting to be taken down to the tracks to catch mice, but Subway Pete had other plans. I soon found myself sitting alongside Subway Pete beside a park bench on which a bedraggled old tramp lay sound asleep. I stared and sniffed curiously while Subway Pete jumped nimbly onto the bench and began to meow plaintively. The old man stirred and then peered blearily from half-open eyes. He mumbled to himself, shuffled further over and tried to resume his nap. His hair was matted and greasy and there was a one-centimeter stubble on his blotchy face.

There was staleness and decay in his body odor, but I noticed some pleasant food smells as well. I waited curiously to see if he would wake up and offer us something to eat.

Subway Pete continued to meow and even rubbed up against the old man's shoulder. This time the tramp grunted and slowly roused himself to a sitting position. He peered at us, frowning gruffly, then smiled and spoke quite kindly. "Well, well, so ya' brought along a new friend today, huh? Well, ain't he a purty one."

The old man scratched affectionately behind Subway Pete's ears and grinned as the cat purred in response. Then he began opening and rummaging around in his bags for food scraps. I did not care much for the cold fries but ate them anyway. Next, the old man tossed some slightly stale meat scraps to me and I wolfed them down ravenously. Subway Pete ate lazily, obviously having been fed earlier by the tramp. The man watched me eat and remarked, "Ho, he's a hungry one now, ain't he? Here boys, I got a special treat for both of youse."

With that, he scrounged into another of his many bags and brought out a tin of sardines. Even Subway Pete got excited and the tramp had to divide the fish evenly so we wouldn't scrap over the tin. I gobbled my fish quickly so I could beat Subway Pete to the tin to lick the fish oil and remaining fish particles. The man chuckled as he watched us eat. Then he chuckled again. "Ain't nothin' more satisfyin' then a full belly, huh, boys?"

Subway Pete rubbed against the old man's legs purring contentedly but I sat out of reach, preferring just to purr my appreciation. One could never be too careful. The old fellow seemed harmless enough, but if people paid "big bucks" for Siamese I wasn't going to take a chance on being nabbed by him to be sold cheap to one of his cat-loving buddies.

The old man resettled himself on the bench and went back to sleep, leaving us to wash up after dinner. I noticed that Subway Pete stopped now and again while he was grooming to scratch or chew at certain spots on his body. He caught me looking at him and grinned in that crooked way of his. "Fleas," he explained. "Bloody little pests! You'll soon be infested too. There's a pretty bad epidemic this year."

The moment he said that, I was absolutely positive I felt several of them crawling in my fur. I decided to change the subject. "Where are those fabulous food smells coming from?"

"Oh, those," answered Subway Pete. "That's Harry's Diner. It's a great hangout. Not like a lot of restaurants where the owners threaten to kill ya for just begging food scraps. The fat guy that owns the place, Harry Wilkes, he's a real cat-lover. Him and his kid Angie love all cats, even Ugly Ben, but Mrs. Wilkes is one o' them high-class snobs who takes her Siamese cat around to these fancy cat shows and forbids the snooty thing so much as to speak to us commoners. She's the sort that bats stray cats off the steps with her broom."

I gulped when he said this and was glad I had not told him anything about my "fancy cat show" family. I was curious about Harry and was glad when Subway Pete continued gossiping about his family.

"Mrs. Snoot-box forbids her kid to touch any of us strays, but Angie makes friends with us on the sly. They live just a few blocks past the park – real classy place. And that cat of theirs, I've never seen anything like it. Siamese like you – but a total snob. They call her Simcha. Thinks she's too good for all us common fellows 'cause she's a big deal show cat and TV star. The kid takes this Simcha chick for walks around the block sometimes. You oughta' see it. I'll take ya' up there some time. Simcha has this diamond-studded collar and fancy leash and walks around like some sort of queen with her nose in the air. It's really weird, man. You just gotta see her."

I realized with a pang that I would have eventually met her, not as a despised stray but as a fellow showcat and competitor. Subway Pete noticed my sad expression and commented, "Missing home, huh? I'll bet you had it good."

"I did, I did," I murmured humbly, "and I'll never take Frank and Lorna or my parents for granted again!"

"Yeah, if you ever see them again," he replied sympathetically. "C'mon, let's head over to Harry's. Meet the gang. They're usually there about now. Maybe they can give us some advice about finding your family."

This suggestion cheered me up somewhat as I followed him to the diner. As we made our way through the park and along grubby back lanes, I tried to thank Subway Pete for his kindness.

He laughed and joked, "Listen kid, with my savvy and your good looks, we'll make us quite a team. We'll get the juiciest meat scraps. Just remember me—your good old buddy—okay?"

I smiled and promised earnestly that I would.

"And if you don't find your folks again, I'll teach you the ropes and introduce you to the right cats. I'll warn you who to watch out for too. You already know about Nasty Joe; we'll take you around to his place and point out him and his van. And Big Tom is bad news too. He's the meanest tom for miles around. You wanna steer clear of him and his crowd. You're lucky it was me and my lot in the park tonight. When Big Tom and his gang are in there, you stay out and I mean out with a capital 'O'—got it?"

"Yes," I replied meekly, longing for my safe, sheltered home.

"I'll teach you how to scrounge for food. You can't count on the old tramp. He sometimes disappears for weeks. Tomorrow noon we'll have us a mousing run and check out some good grub sources. There's lotsa places where it's not safe to scrounge. Some people put out poison or let their dogs out on you and you gotta' stay out of Big Tom's territory or he'll kill ya. Then there's Nasty Joe's traps. You get caught in one o' his traps and it's game over. Like I say, kid, stick with me and you oughta make out all right."

I had a few embarrassing moments trying to keep up with Subway Pete. For one thing, he's an incredible jumper. From a sitting position he can leap to the top of a two-meter fence as effortlessly as a gliding bird. I missed my first try and had to back up and take a running start. Even when I did make it to the top I practically toppled off and made a total fool of myself scrabbling around to secure my position. Subway Pete just sat there grinning. "Practice – that's what it takes. I've been this route hundreds of times. You'll learn."

We squeezed through a narrow gap between two buildings and I stepped out into the weed-entangled lot in back of Harry's. The food smells were tantalizing. I was so taken up with them when I first arrived that I did not even notice the other cats sitting around the cluttered lot. No one took much notice of us so I was able to perch on top of an empty lettuce crate and observe the gang. Most of them were busy with grooming and a couple were napping. It was actually a rather peaceful scene. I wondered if they would all start scrapping when the food was tossed out.

Chapter Four

The first cat to speak up was a dainty calico. She was sitting on a rusty, overturned freezer that was missing a door. She glanced coyly in my direction as she asked Subway Pete, "Who's your new friend – prrrrr?"

Subway Pete just ignored her. He hopped onto a plastic milk crate, stretched vigorously and yawned.

"Name's Shalom," I said.

"And I'm Miss Calico," she cooed.

"Nice to meet you," I replied politely.

"Me oh my," croaked a homely, battle-scarred stray, "what brings fancy Mr. Siam down to our neck o' the woods?"

I knew without being told that this was Ugly Ben. I found his rudeness annoying. I replied irritably, "I have a right to roam where I please, thank you very much!"

"Woooo – rowrr," teased a beautiful, long-haired white cat. "He's a touchy one." She was seated near a dignified, silver tabby on top of another lettuce crate. She looked at me with wide emerald-green eyes and explained, "Ugly Ben really is an old sweetie, my dear. The arthritis makes him a bit cantankerous and he's getting on in years but he's worth his weight in catnip. My name is Pretty Sal and this handsome fellow on my right is Doc Jones."

Doc Jones just nodded politely.

"And up there on the roof we have Preacher Ted. Wake up Preach – we got company!"

Perched atop a low shed sheltered by a large tree, the big black cat was almost invisible in the darkening shadows. I gazed intently up at him. Preacher Ted opened his luminous green eyes and looked me over briefly.

"Cool man," he replied with a Southern drawl. "Call me when dinnah's served." Then he closed his eyes again.

Another cat spoke. "My name's Truckin' Sam and this here's my little sweetie, Timid Gray." Truckin' Sam and Timid Gray were seated on a large tree stump, tucked cosily beside each other. The golden-eyed gray suited her name but I was curious why the husky orange tabby was called Truckin' Sam. Truckin' Sam looked me over curiously as he asked, "Where d'ya hang yer hat, kid?"

"He's lost," Subway Pete replied.

"Tough break," Truckin' Sam responded. "How'd it happen?"

I told them my story but left out the part about my show cat connections. Everyone but Ugly Ben looked sympathetic. He just sat with half-open eyes, wheezing asthmatically.

"A good-lookin' fellow like you shouldn't have any problem finding a new home," said Miss Calico with a flirtatious smile. "Why, I know all sorts of people who'd take me in if I was the settling kind."

"He's not a silly gad-a-bout like you," said Subway Pete. "He wants to get back with his own family."

Miss Calico ignored the criticism and continued to smile prettily at all of us. Preacher Ted stood up and yawned hugely, then sat down to scratch and chew at some new flea bites. "It's enough to drive a saint to swearin'," he hissed. Several cats grinned sympathetically. Then he asked Truckin' Sam, "So how was your last truckin' run, Sam?"

"Man—you guys woulda loved it," said Truckin' Sam. "Me and my truck-driving buddy are king o' the road. What a life! Eatin' and sleepin' all the way to Vancouver and back. Ernie stops at all the best truckin' stops, and let me tell you—there's no hangin' out back a' those restaurants beggin' for scraps. No man! I eat high off the hog on those truckin' runs. There's even been a time or two they let me in the restaurant."

"In? Right inside?" asked Subway Pete in amazement.

"Yuppers!"

"Hey man," exclaimed Preacher Ted, "yo' shore done struck pay dirt when y'all latched onto that truck driver."

"He latched onto me, boys. Cats like me are the independent type. I been footloose and fancy-free too long. I'd go mad locked up all day in some sweet little old lady's apartment with nothin' to do and nowhere to go. Man, I love the open highways and so does my buddy, Ernie. He's a man after my own heart. He lets me run loose at the truck stops and whistles me in when it's time to go."

Miss Calico sighed romantically and was flashed a warning look from Timid Gray. Truckin' Sam gazed keenly at me and advised, "If you don't hitch up with your folks again, little feller, you choose your new family carefully. Don't latch onto the first person that comes along just 'cause he's a free meal wagon."

Subway Pete winked at me and I smiled as I recalled my first "meal wagon."

Truckin' Sam continued, "Those prairie winters are wicked though. I don't do much chasin' around when it's 40 below zero and blowin' like the devil. It's a tough life for the prairie barn cats. I met up with this old tom at one of our favorite truck stops near Moose Jaw. The farm where he's stayin' lost darn near half its cat population last winter. Some fifteen or sixteen cats froze to death. You guys think you got something to bellyache about in winter? Those poor farm cats got it rough. The old tom says the farmer lets his cats breed a lot so's there'll be plenty left over for mousers in the spring."

"That's awful," said Pretty Sal. "I'm sure they could rig up something in the barn for the poor old things."

"Well – maybe some o' the farmers do. I'm just goin' by what that one old tom was telling me."

"Some people are terribly thoughtless," said Timid Gray. This was the first time she had spoken and she fell silent immediately after. I sensed she had been given reason to fear humans and wondered what had made her such a timid, mistrustful cat.

"Thoughtless is not the word for it," said Doc Jones. "There's some that are downright cruel."

"Oh please, let's not talk about it," cried Miss Calico. "It upsets me so when you start into your horrid tales about animal abuse."

"Furbrain," mumbled Ugly Ben under his breath.

If Miss Calico heard the insult, she just ignored it.

"Speaking of animal abuse, have you warned the kid about Nasty Joe?" asked Doc Jones.

The mention of Nasty Joe's name was met by a round of snarls and hisses from the group.

"You better believe it!" exclaimed Subway Pete.

Preacher Ted spoke up next. "Ah tells ya', young feller, there's a few of us has had some narrow escapes and we is wise to his ways. If he gits his wicked ol' hands on yer body, yo' is dead meat! He hates cats – all cats!"

Subway Pete warned sternly, "Like I said, he killed one of my best buddies. There's a couple others I suspect he's done in but I know for sure he killed Chalkie. Timid Gray saw him do it!"

Timid Gray shuddered visibly and hunched her body into a tight ball as though to keep out a wintry chill. I glanced at Subway Pete as he nodded. Several cats glanced compassionately in her direction.

Truckin' Sam spoke up next. "The guy's a nut case. He nabbed a local strays one night along with Timid Gray and Chalkie. Timid Gray was the only one to make it back, but hopefully the other cat escaped too. Timid Gray didn't hang around long enough to find out."

Ugly Ben commented bitterly, "I wish some people would round up Nasty Joe and use him for target practice in the garbage dump. Let him know the sheer, stark terror of being shot at and hit time and again while you're running for your life!"

Timid Gray shuddered again and there was silence. Then she spoke mournfully, "He must have fired three or four bullets into poor Chalkie before he killed him. It was so ghastly . . . oh . . . I still have nightmares about Chalkie screaming and running and stumbling and. . .." Timid Gray's voice rose in a sorrowful wail and Pretty Sal hurried to her side, murmuring words of comfort while Doc Jones reassured her. "I'm sure someone will put an end to his madness. He'll be caught one day, and we homeless cats will be able to walk the streets again without fear."

"Are all of you . . . uh . . . homeless?" I asked.

They glanced at each other with amused grins and I feared I had asked a silly question. But they responded in good humor.

"Well now, the truck's as much of a home as I'll ever want," said Truckin' Sam.

"I belong to the vet that runs the Animal Care Clinic a few blocks north of the diner," said Doc Jones. "My owner brought me in two summers ago and never came back. Still don't know what became of him but I've been at the clinic ever since."

"Ah'm not too bad off neither," said Preacher Ted. "They let me hang 'round the local parsonage to catch mice and ah gets fed reg'lar in return. Don't really belong to no one in partic'lar, but often wishes ah did."

"Me too," sighed Subway Pete.

"I'm too old and ugly. No one would want me," grumbled Ugly Ben.

"I would love a home too but it would break my heart if it meant leaving Doc," said Pretty Sal.

"It's different with me," said Timid Gray. "I ran off on my owners. All they did was quarrel and fight. They sometimes took their meanness out on me and usually forgot to feed me. I'm not much worse off being a stray."

"Well, I can have a home any old time I please but I'm a free spirit," said Miss Calico. She looked at me in her coy way again and asked, "Isn't that why you ran off? You wanted to be a free spirit too?"

Ugly Ben snorted irritably. "Sure he did, but not on a permanent basis. And as for you, Miss Free Spirit, you'll eat those words when you're old and battle-worn and nobody wants you anymore. You'll be sorry you turned up that purty little nose at all the kind folks that tried to give you a home." Ugly Ben advised me, "Don't count on being found, boy. Most strays aren't that lucky. You gotta think about survival, ya hear? Maybe try to find yourself a new home if your folks don't turn up soon. . .."

Suddenly a clattering noise near the back of the restaurant charged the cats into frenzied action. Everyone darted straight to the old wooden steps and waited in tense anticipation. The thumping and clattering came nearer the door. Then the door flew open and Harry appeared on the porch with an armload of empty cardboard boxes and a pail dangling from one arm. A massive wave of exquisite food odors flowed through the open door as all of us sniffed the air, our noses twitching eagerly. He tossed the boxes into the garbage compactor, then stood with a big grin, holding the bucket up in the air. I could tell this was a traditional routine by the way everyone responded. Miss Calico and Subway Pete rubbed along his legs, Truckin' Sam reared up and actually stood on his hind legs meowing aggressively while Doc Jones and Preacher Ted paced back and forth, eyes intent on Harry's face and the pail of food. Pretty Sal sat on the porch meowing daintily, waving her fluffy white tail as she gazed unwaveringly at Harry Wilkes's jovial face. Timid Gray and I sat politely on the outskirts with Ugly Ben who meowed like a croaking frog.

I looked at him in surprise and he grinned. "Froze the old vocal chords last winter," he explained. "Now I meow like a Siamese."

"Rah-owrrrr," I replied and he grinned again.

My distinctive meow attracted Mr. Wilkes's attention and he stared at me in surprise. "Well, I'll be!" he exclaimed. "Where did that fellow come from?"

I shifted uneasily but did not scamper away. He tossed the meat scraps among the cats, starting with those nearest. I did not gobble my portion right away but stopped to investigate the human scents first.

"Don't waste your time scenting it, boy," advised Ugly Ben, "or you'll lose it. Us strays ain't very polite, especially when the pickin's are slim."

I chewed quickly, keeping a careful eye on Mr. Wilkes who seemed very interested in me. He stood, hands on hips, smiling with satisfaction as we gobbled our food. Then he turned to the door and called, "Hey Carl, come get a look at this Siamese." I backed away slightly when another man appeared in the doorway.

Mr. Wilkes scratched his head in puzzlement, "Whose do ya think he is?"

"Dunno," the taller man shrugged, "but they're dumb to let him run loose. Somebody will pinch him fer sure."

"I'm tempted myself," chuckled Mr. Wilkes.

When the men turned back into the restaurant I resumed eating. Once they were finished eating, the cats left one by one until Subway Pete and I were on our own.

"Well buddy, you want a new home?" he asked. "I'll take ya' around to Wilkes's place; you hang around for a couple days so that he and Angie know yer lost and I'll betcha ten-to-one they take you right in. Talk about posh livin', boy—you'll have it made!"

"Right—and then for sure I'll never see my own family again. No thanks. I just want to get back home. That's all I care about. I don't like the idea of living in the same house as a smart-aleck showcat who thinks she's the cat's meow."

"'Cat's meow' – ha, that's a good one!" laughed Subway Pete. "C'mon sport, let's check out the place anyway. Sometimes Wilkes's kid tosses me a few grub treats when she's walkin' Simcha."

"I'm not hungry anymore," I replied.

"Never, never turn down food," joked Subway Pete. "Eat till yer guts pop, man, 'cause ya' never know when your next meal's coming. There's the odd night Harry forgets us, besides which he's not there weekends. You gotta pile on the fat in the summer 'cause you'll need it come winter when the pickin's get scarce. What if you're not found? We gotta prepare for the worst. You're still a kid – you gotta lot to learn about survival. You're lucky ya' got me so you don't have to learn everything the hard way."

"I'm really grateful, Subway Pete," I exclaimed, "I really am."

"Sure, kid, sure. Let's go!"

Chapter Five

We wasted no time getting to the Wilkes's home a few blocks off Yonge in a quiet, exclusive residential area. I wanted to sniff and explore along the way but Subway Pete was impatient to get there. I noticed it was getting darker.

"Angie usually comes out around now to walk Simcha so don't dawdle," he advised.

The street was lined with majestic trees and beautiful homes. The Wilkes's house and its large yard were nearly hidden by the tall, stately shrubs that grew all around it. Big wrought-iron gates blocked the entrance to the sidewalk and driveway. The two-story house was three times the size of my own home and much more elegant. It seemed to have a hundred windows, all invitingly lit, giving us glimpses of the luxury inside. Subway Pete was not interested in going inside the gate but we poked our heads through the railing to get a better look.

The yard was like a small park. The first thing that caught my eyes was the lily-covered fish pond. I had never seen one before, but Mother had described them and I wondered if this one contained any goldfish.

A cobblestone walk led off to an arbored patio with white wicker patio furnishings and a variety of potted plants. I admired the beautifully cultivated flowers and trees in the yard and wished Subway Pete would go inside with me to explore everything more closely. He seemed to read my thoughts as he informed me, "Strays aren't welcome in there. You wait till after dark when Angie's mother is not around to bat you off the place with her broom." He stopped and tilted his head to one side. "Listen, ya' hear that piano?"

I perked my ears forward to catch the sound and he explained, "Angie's practicing. She always comes out with Simcha for her walk after she's done. Won't be long now."

Both of us sat on the walk cleaning ourselves as we waited. I took special care with my grooming as I thought about Simcha, the "fancy showcat." I did not intend to look like a scruffy stray for our first encounter. Subway Pete noticed my fussing and smirked but said nothing.

Suddenly he stopped grooming and stiffened, one paw suspended in midair. "Bad news," he hissed. "Big Tom's headed our way. He's wild about that Simcha chick. He's not gonna be pleased about us hangin' around."

I followed Subway Pete's gaze down the street and noticed a hefty-sized orange tom sitting under a street lamp. For a minute the three of us sat motionless, eyeing one another. Subway Pete's paw was still extended in a handshake gesture but the fur along his back began to bristle. At first Big Tom sat like a statue, his unblinking gaze riveted in our direction. The overhead streetlight reflected in his yellow eyes making them gleam with a strange electric glow. The tip of his tail began to twitch irritably and his eyes narrowed.

He lowered his head, and stared even harder as he began advancing slowly toward us. He crept stealthily along the walk until he was almost directly across the road from us. He was every bit the battered, battle-scarred tom that Subway Pete had described. The bulldog toughness in his big muscular body was absolutely intimidating. I would have turned tail and run if Subway Pete had not been right beside me. Big Tom's defiant eyes slid contemptuously back and forth between the two of us while his tail whipped angrily back and forth.

One of his ears was ragged and torn and there were scars on his face and head. Several tufts of fur were missing around his neck from recent cat fights. He seemed to double in size as his fur bristled and stood on end. As he began edging slowly across the road, all of us arched our backs, rearing our bodies to maximum height on fully stretched legs. Our ears flattened in anger. The wicked-looking tom's caterwauling was savagely hostile but Subway Pete and I were not to be outdone as we growled and moaned threateningly in return.

"Naughty puss-cats! Now you stop that right now!"

I was so startled by the sudden, unexpected human voice that I jumped and hissed in surprise. I turned to face a slender young girl, holding in her arms the most beautiful Siamese I had ever seen.

Simcha gazed coolly at us with deep, clear blue, almond-shaped eyes. The jeweled collar glimmered in the streetlight. Her long, slender body was draped regal and elegant on her mistress's arm and her short sleek fur shimmered silvery highlights under the street lamp's glow. Her ears, feet, tail and delicate face were a lovely bluish-gray. The rest of her body was white with an enchanting blue tinge.

"Are you fellows going to behave yourselves now?" asked Angie. There was a teasing sparkle in her lively brown eyes. She was an agreeable person in spite of the scolding tone in her voice.

A mass of natural brown curls framed her freckled boyish face. Her friendly smile reminded me of her father Harry. I guessed she was around eleven and sensed she was not that nuisance sort of child who stuffs you under the covers at night or ties shoelaces on your tail to tease you. I liked her immediately.

Simcha continued to watch us, her wide blue eyes studying each of us in turn. I could well imagine this descendent of the royal cats of Siam living in the palaces and temples of Siam. Her gaze, princess-like and aloof, held me in spellbound silence.

Angie began strolling down the sidewalk holding Simcha in her arms. Subway Pete darted after Angie, purring and rubbing against her legs in his usual affectionate way while I tagged along behind. Big Tom followed alongside on the road, keeping a safe distance from us and gazing admiringly up at Simcha.

The girl leaned over and Simcha sprang gracefully from her arms to the sidewalk. She stood for a moment, waiting for Angie to adjust the leash. She walked with aristocratic dignity by Angie's side. Because Subway Pete was not nearly as much in awe as I was, he began to chat with her in quite a friendly, casual manner. "So, how's business these days? Signed up for any major movies lately?"

Simcha glanced coolly in his direction. "Just a couple of commercials and a few minor movie roles. If anything big comes along, I'll remember the little cats."

"Ohh – rowrrr, fame city here I come," he teased.

Simcha smiled charmingly. "Don't give up the day job."

Big Tom spoke up next. "I say, gorgeous, any chance of you shaking that little security guard of yours?"

Simcha glanced briefly at him with her vivid blue eyes. "Oh my, no. Goodness knows I've tried. I'm afraid we must just go on eating our hearts out at a distance." She sighed mockingly. "Such is the price of fame." She cast a sidelong glance at Big Tom and teased, "Besides, in our circles, love does not enter the picture, for our marriages are . . . " Simcha hesitated delicately " . . . how shall I put it. . .?"

"Arranged?" volunteered an amused Subway Pete.

"Yes, my dear," she purred smoothly, "arranged! And I really don't mind. I much prefer that to the love 'em and leave 'em antics of some modern cats."

Big Tom just grinned boldly and sidled up closer. This annoyed Subway Pete who hissed at him. Angie immediately picked Simcha up and scolded again. "Enough now! I shall have to chase all of you away if you don't settle down."

Subway Pete and I exchanged hostile looks with Big Tom but all of us settled down. In a short while Simcha was allowed to rejoin us in our walk. She seemed amused in a rather disdainful way. "Such naughty fellows," she teased. "I should think you'd all be above scrapping like common alley cats."

"Hey! Hey!" joked Big Tom. "Don't knock it. It's a great life, babe. Ain't got no humans to fence me in. I'm a free cat. I go where I want when I want, see who I want whenever I please – the world is mine to roam at will. You and me together, we could really have a blast!"

"You can't miss what you never had," she replied airily.

Subway Pete snorted scornfully. "Sure, sure, it's a great life. Never know when your next meal's comin', always dodging Animal Control and Nasty Joe, not to mention cat-hating homeowners, mean-tempered toms and malicious children. Then there's wintry blizzards, flea epidemics and poison traps along with frozen ears and tails and rheumatism and disease and . . . " Subway Pete paused with a grin. "But we're free – by George we are free! Mind you, this great freedom does shorten the life span drastically, but such is the price of freedom!"

Simcha stopped and gazed intently at us, but did not comment. Angie stopped too, then sat on the grass and smiled at us. Subway Pete nudged her arm and purred blissfully as she scratched behind his ears. She reached into her jeans and pulled out a small plastic bag. The smell of cat niblets met our noses and we huddled closer in a temporary truce for the tasty treat. Angie fed each of us one at a time, stroking and hugging us repeatedly while Simcha simply sat watching with those fathomless blue eyes. I felt self-conscious under her gaze and tried to cover it up by grooming myself, leaving Big Tom and Subway Pete to gobble the rest of the small biscuits. I pretended to be unconcerned as she looked me over, measuring and judging me with the practical eye of an experienced show cat. Inside however, I felt greatly ill at ease. Whatever was she thinking? Did she think I was a stray too? Or did she think I lived somewhere in her neighborhood in some luxurious mansion with people at my beck and call?

"Oh darling things," crooned Angie, "I wish you could all come and live with me." She looked at me and reached out to stroke my fur. It felt good to be petted again and I purred, allowing her to pick me up and settle me on her lap. I sighed longingly as she continued to stroke me and scratch around my ears. "Isn't he gorgeous, Simcha?" she asked. "I wonder who he belongs to?"

"Where do you live?" asked Simcha.

It was on the tip of my tongue to lie and pretend I belonged somewhere in her beautiful neighborhood, but Subway Pete spoke up. "He's lost, poor kid. Been lost for two days."

I could have scratched his nose. I refused to meet Simcha's eyes and see her pitying look.

"That's most unfortunate," Simcha responded.

"Heck no! It's a great life," said Big Tom. "Isn't it, kid?"

"It has its good points," I responded wryly, "but I would prefer to be with my family."

"Suck!" scorned Big Tom under his breath.

Subway Pete's fur began to bristle and Simcha warned, "Cool it, fellows. I don't fancy a premature end to my evening walk because of your silly scrapping."

Needless to say, we meekly obeyed.

Big Tom continued to amuse Simcha with his flirtatious banter. Angie seemed to think he was quite a charming cat and I had to admit he had a real way with people. He nudged and purred around Angie, meowing enthusiastically, rolling on the ground beside her and then licking at her hands.

Big Tom's parting words that evening (out of Simcha's hearing, of course) promised certain death if he ever caught us hanging around Simcha's place again!

Chapter Six

"I'm ashamed of you," teased Subway Pete as we ambled back toward Yonge Street. "Every cat this end of Toronto is in love with that Siamese chick. I expected better of you!"

"She doesn't even know my name," I replied sadly.

"No wonder, you hardly said two words to her tonight. Cat got your tongue? Meowrrr?"

"Funny. Really funny."

"Cheer up, kid. We'll go see her again tomorrow night."

I stopped dead in my tracks, plopped down on the sidewalk and stared at him in bewilderment. "But . . . but Big Tom . . . " I stammered.

"Look kid. I told ya – stick with me. You think I survived this long on good looks and luck? Think again. Big Tom's no prob, kid, no prob."

"But . . . you think she's a snob. You said. . . ."

"So? Big deal! I like excitement, man, and I don't like Big Tom. We're gonna give Big Tom a run for his money. He's got his nerve pushin' us around. That cat's nose is really gonna be out of joint if Miss Simcha takes a shine to you."

"You're quite a cat, Subway Pete," I laughed.

"I believe you, kid, I believe you. Millions wouldn't but I do. Let's go find a place to bunk down for the night. That's not always an easy job."

The first few places we looked were already occupied by cats who warned us off with everything from a polite meow to a furious growl or hiss. Subway Pete told me that it was far worse trying to get lodgings in winter but I thought this was bad enough. Finally we discovered a toolshed that someone had left open. We crept stealthily inside. We sniffed and looked around before choosing our spot for the night. The shed was full of oil smells and pleasant earth and garden fragrances. I settled into a box of clean rags, turning around several times and sinking gratefully down into the cosy softness. It was quiet except for the faint sounds of the Yonge Street traffic and subway. Subway Pete snuggled down on an old gardening jacket that lay draped over a pile of tires. Both of us yawned widely at the same time and began to wash up for the night.

"I gotta take you mousing soon," said Subway Pete. "Didn't feel like it today 'cause there were too many other interesting things to do and we really struck it lucky with the grub. You gotta keep on top with the mousing though, 'cause if you lose your touch you'll be in for it when food's scarce."

I sighed as I thought of my mother and my safe secure home where a food supply was the least of my worries.

Subway Pete, seeming to guess my thoughts again, was quite sympathetic. "I'm sure your family will do all they can to find you. Meanwhile, you might as well have a blast. Just make sure you steer clear of Nasty Joe. I don't want you to end up like Chalkie."

He continued to warn me about Nasty Joe. "He drives around in this beat-up white van real early in the morning when we're out raiding garbage cans and mousing. He puts out food and traps around his place too but most of us are too smart for him. Oh, by the way, you gotta watch out for the 'coons too."

"'Coons?" I asked.

"Yup! Raccoons. When one of those guys is filling his guts in someone's garbage can, keep your distance till he's good and done. If you see one heading your way, let him have your garbage pickings – I don't care how delicious it is or how hungry you are. Ugly Ben got chewed up by a 'coon once. That's why the poor old guy's so ugly. It's not the toms that messed him up, though heaven knows they did their part. He's had run-ins with some pretty vicious she-cats too!"

Subway Pete paused, then informed me soberly, "Poor old Ugly Ben. I don't reckon he'll make it through the winter. We nearly lost him last year."

We sat quietly, thinking sadly of Ugly Ben's future. Subway Pete spoke up. "Tomorrow I want to show you around the subway. It's a great place for hanging out – lots of action down there. Just don't get yourself flattened by one o' the subway trains. And if we run into a rat tomorrow, you let me handle it. Those jokers are pretty vicious. And just for kicks one of these days we'll take a mouse up onto the subway platform during rush hour. Man, you'll see some action then!"

"You're wild, Subway Pete," I replied laughingly.

He just grinned and changed the subject by teasing, "I bet that Simcha's never caught a mouse in her life."

"She never gets a chance to," I defended.

"Well, maybe we can talk her into giving Wilkes the slip for a couple hours. Take her along on a mousing expedition. I bet that would make your day!"

"Stop your teasing!"

"Sorry!"

I could almost feel Subway Pete grinning in the dark. Suddenly I was struck by an awful thought and lifted my head from my paws to look at Subway Pete's shadowy outline. I asked worriedly, "Subway Pete?"

"Mrrrf?" he replied sleepily.

"What happens to a cat that gets picked up by Animal Control?"

"Don't ask, kid, you don't wanna know. If you're caught by North York Animal Control and don't get sold or claimed in three days, they blink you out!"

"You're right, I don't want to know."

"Mind you, that's not the only animal control agency. Miss Calico got picked up by Public Health Animal Control and, luckily for her, she was sent to the Humane Society."

"How'd she end up around here?"

"Someone from Rosedale bought her, but she ran off. She's cute but she's a real little fishbrain. Ugly Ben can't stand her."

"So I noticed."

Subway Pete yawned again and advised me to get some sleep. "We gotta be out o' here at the crack of dawn. People don't usually mind us being in their sheds and garages but there are exceptions. I made the mistake of bunking down on the nice warm hood of a Roll's Royce once and you shoulda heard the owner cuss me out. I got him back though – it was great!"

I smiled, waiting for him to continue.

"I waited for a rainy day and when he wasn't looking, I sneaked into the garage and left muddy footprints all over his car."

Early the next morning we crept out of the toolshed and stopped to chew some grass, then licked the dew on the lawn. Subway Pete upchucked his grass, but I pretended not to notice. We stalked but missed a robin which flew into a tree and scolded us for our "obnoxious behavior."

We wandered down to the park and found a bench to sit on, letting the sun warm our bodies as we washed up. It was a beautiful day and I felt encouraged. I was also very excited about my first hunting trip. Several pigeons eyed us suspiciously as we made our way toward a solid guard-rail fence that ran along the foot of the embankment beside the tracks. Subway Pete led me down the embankment to a place where an opening had been dug beneath the fence and we wriggled through to the opposite side. I sniffed timidly at the opening, then squeezed through. I trembled as the first train thundered past. I had grown used to their rumbling while I was in the park, but they seemed monstrously loud at such close range and shook the ground under my feet. I crouched close to the earth, ears flattened as the first one passed by, but after a while I looked up as they passed. There were not many people inside the cars although Subway Pete assured me the cars would soon be packed full for the rush hour.

I trembled with excitement as we scented our way along the embankment. Though I had never smelled a mouse before, I knew immediately which odors were left by the mice. I darted here and there, following various trails. Subway Pete did not waste his time running about, but watched the tracks and plant growth along the embankment with an intent and practiced eye. Suddenly he tensed, crouched down and froze, his gaze fixed straight ahead. I watched carefully and eventually detected a slight tremor in the weeds some three meters ahead of him. The tremor stopped and started at intervals along the mouse's path as the rodent hesitated now and again to eat or scent its surroundings.

It seemed to take Subway Pete forever to stalk the mouse but in reality it took no more then a couple minutes. Just as another subway car rumbled into view, he leapt and pounced on the mouse. The train distracted me and I glanced nervously up as it flew by.

I was watching the last car pass by when a tiny flurry on the tracks behind the passing train caught my eye. A mouse! A small, gray mouse! In two giant leaps I was on the track, pouncing and leaping around in mad pursuit after the mouse until I finally caught it.

Before another hour passed, we caught and ate several mice. Subway Pete shook his head admiringly as we sat on a park bench to groom ourselves and said, "I would've never believed in a million years that you've never caught a mouse before. You Siamese are hunters with a capital 'H.' Wow, man, that pouncing leap is out of sight. With a bit of practice you'll hit it dead-on every time. Just make sure you do your pouncing on those tracks after the train goes by, not before. I know a cat that got so excited over this mouse he was chasing, he didn't notice the train until it was almost too late."

"His name wouldn't have been Subway Pete by any chance?" I asked.

Subway Pete grinned impishly but did not reply.

Chapter Seven

We spent a pleasant morning in the park, napping in the sun and visiting with several people. The old tramp wandered by just before lunch and gave us several handfuls of dry cat food. He ate some of it himself which surprised me immensely. When I mentioned this to Subway Pete, he did not see what was so strange about a human nibbling on cat food.

"We eat human food too, don't we? Maybe he saves money by eating cat food. I find it rather reassuring to see a human eating our food. That prove's it's healthy for us to eat, don't you think?"

"But . . . but, that's weird," I said. "The old guy is weird."

Subway Pete just laughed and joked, "Welcome to Toronto, boy. Stick with me and you'll meet some people that are really weird."

We hung around during the lunch hour begging from people who came to spend their lunch break in the park, but took off when Big Tom and some of his tough-looking friends appeared."

"I'll fight 'em for food if I'm really hungry," said Subway Pete, "but there's no point squabbling just for the sake of fighting."

I certainly agreed with this. The last thing I needed was a torn ear or scarred face. As a showcat, I would be totally ruined so I was most anxious to stay out of trouble.

For a while we wandered around, exploring just for the fun of it. Several times we met one or more of the gang and exchanged some local gossip. Pretty Sal informed us shyly that she was "in the family way" and we congratulated her very enthusiastically. Doc Jones beamed proudly and said he hoped they would all turn out to be as beautiful as their mother.

As they walked away, Subway Pete commented, "Stray mothers don't have an easy go of it, but they are incredibly resourceful and mighty courageous as well. Pretty Sal is a gracious lady, my boy, but she's a real fighter too. I've seen her send some mighty tough-looking cats on the run!"

Later that day we made our way to Nasty Joe's place. I was frightened and Subway Pete seemed nervous too as we crept along the lane behind his house.

"You pay close attention now," he warned. "I'm gonna show you where not to hang around or scrounge for food. Nasty Joe keeps moving the traps around and using different kinds of traps. Far as I know he's got at least three of them and they aren't always on his own property. Sometimes he hides them along the lane or in his garage and there's the odd time he's sneaked one under his neighbor's shrubs. There's nothing more pitiful on the face of this earth than to see a cat in one of those cages. You know the poor cat is doomed and he or she does too. It's so sad. They sit there with huge frightened eyes, meowing in the most pitiful way. At least the traps are humane because Nasty Joe knows he'd get in huge trouble if someone found out and complained about animals suffering in the traps."

"Why don't they complain about him trapping cats?" I asked.

"Oh, there are lots of folks who use traps for catching strays. It's quite legal, but it's not legal to kill off the strays yourself. They don't know that Nasty Joe is doing that."

"He has to be stopped!" I exclaimed.

"Yeah, that's what all the cats say. We've racked our brains trying to figure out a way to stop him – but we're only cats. What can we do?"

"He's must be stopped!" I hissed.

"Well, let us know if you get any brain waves. Even Big Tom would cooperate if you came up with a good plan. He's lost a few of his buddies too. Let's go see the garage first. He always leaves the side door open so us cats will wander in and get caught in the trap he keeps inside."

Subway Pete showed me around the large garage and I nervously sniffed about. The rust-spotted white van was parked to one side of the garage and I scented it carefully. I also scented the odor left on the other side of the garage by the tires of Nasty Joe's car. There was an empty cage along one wall with some savory meat scraps inside. We sat studying the wood and wire mesh cage.

"How does it work?" I whispered, as though Nasty Joe might hear.

"I've never seen how it traps you, but Timid Gray said the upraised gate slammed down when she started to eat so I reckon it's connected somehow with the food. Or maybe it depends where you step. Beats me."

I sniffed fearfully at the cage, edging past it slowly and keeping a healthy distance away.

"Jumpin' catfish! Did you hear that?" Subway Pete exclaimed suddenly.

I hissed out of pure fright and the fur bristled along my whole body. Then Subway Pete laughed. "Settle down, it's not Nasty Joe. Listen! See if you can hear it too!"

"What?" I gasped. "What are you talking about? You scared me half to death!"

"That whimpering," he said. "I could swear I heard something whimpering. C'mon—let's investigate!"

Subway Pete scurried out the door and darted underneath a hedge. I followed quickly. We sat, huddled together, gazing around the yard. One of Nasty Joe's traps stood in plain view beside his house but there was nothing in it. Our ears pricked forward in the same direction, as a faint but distinct whimper reached us from the sun porch. We stared at the open screen door waiting to hear the whimper again.

"Something caught?" I asked.

"Yeah, but it's sure not a cat. We gotta check this out. Sounds like it's over in the sun porch."

We crept silently along the shrubs until we reached the house. Then we heard a whining sound, followed by a scratching noise. Seconds later, we both stood tensed for flight but peering cautiously inside the sun room. We saw the cage immediately, but it most certainly did not contain a mournful-eyed stray cat. I almost had to smile at the fluffy-eared gangly pup that sat with his nose pressed hopefully against the wire netting. As we drew close to the cage, he yelped excitedly and pounced against the wire.

"Hush up now!" Subway Pete warned sternly.

The red-haired hunting pup sat down, looking expectantly at us with his clear, bright brown eyes.

"You got yourself in a fine pickle, junior," said Subway Pete. "Where's your ma?"

"I don't think she knows I'm gone. We live down near the end of the street – maybe five or six houses. Oh, please get my mother! Please? I'm sure she'll know how to get me out of this horrible thing!"

"What's your name?" I asked.

"Muffy. They call me Muffy. And my mother's name is Cinnamon but everyone calls her Cindy. Oh, please get my mother."

Subway Pete looked at me and nodded. "We better head over right away. You say it's five or six houses down?"

The pup smiled winsomely and nodded. Subway Pete reassured him that everything would be all right as we set off at a run. We picked up several dog scents which was rather confusing until we found one that had a bit of the pup's scent mingled in. We traced the odor to the pup's backyard and then slowed to a cautious walk. We were not quite sure how Cindy would receive us but need not have worried. She was sniffing anxiously around the yard and the instant she saw us she asked if we had seen her little son. Her beautiful, dark eyes grew wide with alarm when we told her what had happened. Several other pups were tumbling about in front of their doghouse. She warned them with a low, rumbling growl to get into the house and "stay put" until she returned. Then we all rushed off for Nasty Joe's.

Cindy worked desperately to free her son, pushing,

pawing and chewing at the cage, but to no avail. The pup's eyes grew huge with alarm and he trembled with fear. I felt desperately sorry for both of them and wondered what would become of him if Nasty Joe should suddenly appear. I wanted to ask Subway Pete, but did not dare say anything in front of the dogs.

Finally, panting with fright and exertion, Cindy cried out, "I've got to get Mark and Helen. Pray someone is still home. Please stay here and calm my little baby. I'll be back as soon as I can."

By now the pup was frantic and would have set up a noisy howl if Subway Pete had not cautioned him again to be quiet. We chatted with him and tried to be amusing as we waited for Mark and Helen to arrive. I poked my paws through the wire and patted playfully at him, while Subway Pete rubbed along the side of the cage and poked his nose through one of the openings. Muffy smiled affectionately at Subway Pete's nose, then sat down, tongue lolling out in friendly fashion. His eyes followed our every move. We could hear Cindy barking and detected the sound of a person running along the lane with her. We darted toward the door when they arrived in the yard, preparing to run off, but Muffy pleaded, "Oh, please stay. You mustn't leave. Mother would be so disappointed."

We paced nervously as Muffy's mistress entered the room, but the lady had eyes only for Muffy. "Good heavens!" she exploded angrily. "What on earth is going on here?"

Muffy went into an ecstatic fit, pouncing at the cage and trying to lick Helen's fingers through the wire. For several tense moments the lady fumbled with the door. She finally flung it open, quickly reaching in to snatch the pup to safety. She was rewarded with happy barking and face-licking by both Mother and son. We sat by, smiling and purring delightedly.

"Please come along with us," said Cindy. "Join us for a bite to eat, won't you? I want to thank you for your help and introduce you to the rest of the family."

"I never need to be asked twice when food's involved," joked Subway Pete, and we set off eagerly for Cindy's house.

Helen stopped to examine the trap in the yard and frowned. "What is going on around here," she asked again. "I shall have to get Mark to look into this."

She hurried out of the yard and did not slow her step until we were safely off the property.

"Our owners adore animals," said Cindy. "You needn't feel shy around them. Their names are Mark and Helen Armstrong. We have two adopted stray cats as well."

"And you'll like my brothers and sisters," added Muffy.

Helen cuddled the squirming Muffy securely in her arms until we reached their yard, then she set him on the ground where he was enveloped by a happy, writhing bundle of relieved brothers and sisters. We were amused to learn that the five pups were named Muffy, Ruffy, Tuffy, Duffy and Puffy. Cindy lay down with Muffy on the cement patio, licking away the odious scent of Nasty Joe's cage. We sat nearby waiting for dinner, telling Cindy everything we knew about Nasty Joe. Cindy agreed emphatically that Nasty Joe's murderous rampages had to be stopped.

"I should imagine that the municipality has reported this problem to the Humane Society's abuse investigators if the poor creatures are being found shot. They will not rest until the man is found and charged. We must think of some way to expose that horrid man. If only we could tell our owners somehow."

She smiled and looked kindly into our eyes as she concluded, "I can't express how grateful I am to you!"

We smiled and purred happily. The food was delicious and we ate far too much, especially Subway Pete. Helen stroked us lovingly and made us feel very welcome. The adopted strays smiled encouragingly as we ate, for they knew how much we appreciated being kindly treated and fed. It made me long more than ever for home, enjoying the life of pampered ease I'd taken so much for granted. My future had been so secure – so exciting. But now? I shuddered as I thought of Chalkie, running for his life, crying out. Who would be Nasty Joe's next victim?

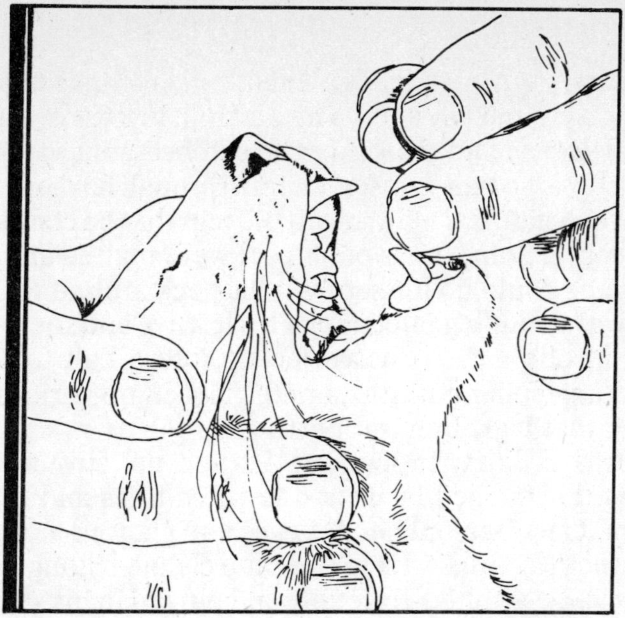

Chapter Eight

"This is awful," I groaned as we climbed atop the shed beside Harry's Diner.

Subway Pete lay down and lifted his head to look at me as he replied amusedly,"Ahhh, the pain of a gut-popping stomach. I love it! Enjoy, my boy, the day may come when it's hunger that's paining our bellies."

He dropped his head again and sighed in deep contentment, purring with pleasure. His stomach was twice its normal size.

We dozed lazily for the rest of that afternoon, waking briefly now and then at unexpected noises or to hiss away unwelcome cats or squirrels. Ugly Ben poked his head over the roof later that day and we invited him to join us. The poor fellow wheezed and groaned as he climbed aboard and tried to wash up for a nap. I observed him through half-open eyes, as he licked halfheartedly at stiff old legs that he could hardly lift anymore. Some areas of his coat were matted and untidy because he could no longer twist his neck around to groom. There was a running infection in his left eye and some recent gashes in one ear. As he curled up into a ball to sleep, I noticed a peculiar guttural sound, glanced up curiously and realized that Ugly Ben was purring!

I was the first to awaken. I stood up, stretching and yawning. I scratched lazily at a few flea bites and began to wash up. Ugly Ben opened his eyes and glanced at me, then closed them again. I walked over and cleaned along his neck and back. He grunted gratefully and purred in his strangled, guttural way. I wandered over to Subway Pete and began to tease him awake.

First I tapped his ear lightly and his tail tip twitched irritably. Then I batted at his tail. The tip twitched more vigorously as I continued to pat and paw at it until finally the entire tail began whipping and thrashing about in annoyance. At this point he woke up and pretended to snarl as he threatened, "I've killed for less than that!"

I just laughed and announced, "Wake up, you lazy furball, we gotta work off some fat before supper."

He sat up and blinked his topaz eyes, then yawned and stretched. He pounced on me for a friendly tussle that woke up Ugly Ben. The old cat snorted irritably and slowly roused himself to a sitting position. "Can't ya' let an old man get some rest? Blast it anyway!"

"Owrowrrr! Sorry Ugly Ben," said Subway Pete. "This

half-grown kitten-friend of mine gets a bit carried away sometimes."

"Sure, blame it all on me," I objected good-naturedly. We sat around gossiping and were gradually joined by other members of the gang. Subway Pete and I were the center of attention that day as we told them about our adventures.

"Imagine a dog being so friendly," commented Doc Jones. "But it does happen now and again. On occasion we get one down at the hospital who doesn't mind cats."

"I bet old Nasty Joe freaked out when he saw that empty cage," laughed Truckin' Sam. "I hope the Armstrongs give that guy a piece of their mind."

"Yeah, I wish there was a way to let Cindy's family know what Nasty Joe is doing," said Subway Pete. "There's no telling what might have happened to her pup and she doesn't intend to let him get away with terrorizing her family or us strays. She says she's gonna see him brought to justice if it's the last thing she does!"

The gang murmured and meowed approval. A short while later, Subway Pete and I set off for Simcha's home.

"Big Tom will be watching out for us this time. We'll have to be mighty wily!" cautioned Subway Pete with his crooked, mischievous grin. I pretended not to be afraid but I was quite worried. It wasn't that I was cowardly, but a torn ear could ruin me as a show cat and it seemed that every second stray had a torn ear.

"I think we could get away with hiding right on the property where it's less likely we'll run into Big Tom," said Subway Pete. "He's pretty scared of Mrs. Wilkes and she hates him with a passion because he's so bold and obnoxious. Mind you, Angie's mother hates all strays. We've nicknamed her the Dragon because she whacks the tar out of you with a broom if she catches you in the yard. She's a real sneak. She creeps up, quieter than a cat, and then whacko! I got me a headache once from her doing that and I know she's caught Big Tom several times."

"Why doesn't she phone Animal Control?" I asked.

"Probably because of Harry and Angie. You wouldn't believe how those dumb strays keep coming back. Simcha just sits in her window and laughs."

"She's not very nice to her fan club, is she?"

Subway Pete laughed. "Local gossip has it that Angie's old lady really goes after Big Tom. Thinks he's the boldest, brassiest thing she's ever seen. She's been heard to say that she'll put a bullet through his head if he doesn't cut out the back fence caterwauling. Man, that guy is really flipped out over Simcha."

"Mrrph," I grumbled. "I don't know what she sees in him!"

"She sure doesn't seem to discourage it," he commented wryly.

We crouched on the ground watching warily as a uniformed servant stepped out onto the big veranda at the back of the house. She ignored us as she walked through the yard to deposit a box of garbage in the back lane. She glanced briefly our way as she strolled back to the house, but otherwise took no notice of us. As she disappeared into the house we could hear Angie starting to practice the piano. She began with some popular rock but switched to classical when her mother told her to "quit fooling around."

"Well, well, look who's come calling!"

We both jumped up at the sound of Simcha's voice.

"Over here, gentlemen. By the kitchen window. Come on up on the veranda. I'll warn you if Mrs. Wilkes comes."

We found Simcha sitting by a large kitchen window and hopped up onto a porch swing near the open screened window. The swing swayed slightly as we leaped up to the spacious window ledge.

She sat on a counter near the window, posed like a beautiful china figurine, with her long tapering tail wound over her forepaws and tucked around her body. I could well imagine her posing for photographers and gazing serenely into TV cameras with her enchanting sapphire blue eyes. I sat, speechless as usual, admiring her elegant form and the satiny coat that shone delicately in the soft light. I could see why cats like Big Tom considered a broom whack on the head a small price to pay for a few moments in her presence. I marveled at the casual, almost careless way that Subway Pete spoke to her.

"You're looking mighty fine tonight, my dear. They been fancying you up for another cat show?"

She laughed softly. "They do fuss horribly over me a week before a show and it makes me a trifle irritable at times.

There's the perpetual grooming and visits to the vet and nail clippings and bathings and probings at my teeth and eyes and ears. Then the salves and conditioners and powderings! And then there's the nuisance of traveling in cages and having strangers stare and prod and heaven-knows-what-all-else!"

"You've got a hard life," joked Subway Pete, "especially since you won that big cat beauty contest."

"What I actually won," she replied loftily, "was the C.F.A. Grand Championship."

"Owwooo," crooned Subway Pete. "Big time stuff hey? Wow! I bet if I ever tried to enter one of those fancy cat shows they'd peg rotten tomatoes at me. How d'ya think my talkative buddy here would make out?"

Simcha's eyes widened with interest. "Where do you come from?" she asked. "Are you . . . uh . . . pedigreed?"

This amused Subway Pete and thoroughly embarrassed me. "Yes," I said simply, hoping she would drop the subject.

"Who are your parents?"

Simcha's clear blue eyes widened in surprise when I told her and she exclaimed excitedly, "Isn't your father a former Grand Champion? I've seen him on the circuit – and doesn't he do some film and modeling? Oh my . . . !"

This time Simcha was at a loss for words!

"Hey! Hey! What gives here?" asked Subway Pete. "Is my buddy some sort of high-fallutin' showcat?"

"Cool it, Subway," I said. "I've never been in a cat show in my life!"

"Yeah?"

"Yeah!"

I glanced sidelong at Subway Pete, fully expecting him to be looking scornfully at me, but instead he looked quite intrigued.

Simcha's eyes shone with excitement. "Oh, you must – you simply must meet Mrs. Wilkes!"

"What?!" hooted Subway Pete. "That dragon! Not on your life!"

"Don't be silly – she'll see at a glance that he's an exceptional cat."

I laughed, "That may be, but poor Subway Pete will get a broom in the butt! That dragon needs to learn that a cat doesn't have to have a fancy pedigree to be something special."

"Hear! Hear!" Subway Pete sang out.

Simcha ignored him and continued admonishing us. "True, but if he does have a pedigree he ought not to waste it. And I'll have you fellows know that large sums of money have been raised by charitable cat shows for cats less fortunate than us."

"Hmmm . . . I see," said Subway Pete. "Well, it looks like you have an even bigger problem then I thought, young fellow. We gotta be careful old Big Tom doesn't chew up those pedigreed ears of yours."

I rolled my eyes heavenward in mock disgust. "Listen, Subway Pete, you don't hear me spouting off about my famous relatives, so quit digging me about my pedigree, okay?"

"Sorry pal," he replied with a winsome smile. "I promise not to hold it against you."

"You're all heart," I replied.

Simcha smiled and stood up to stretch. Just then, Angie's piano playing ceased and she came to prepare Simcha for her walk. She greeted us cheerily through the window and told us to wait as she fetched Simcha's leash and buckled the shimmering collar around her slender neck. The evening was perfect except for Big Tom's presence. As we strolled together, we told Simcha about the adventures we'd had that day. She listened with a look of alarm when we talked about Nasty Joe. She shook her head wonderingly as we told her about Timid Gray's narrow escape and how Chalkie was killed. We told her about the pup we had helped rescue. She thought Cindy and her pups sounded charming and smiled when we described the gang. "I'd love to meet all of them," she said wistfully, "but..."

Angie interrupted our conversation by picking up Simcha and unlatching the front gate. It seemed our time together had only been a few minutes although it had been almost an hour since we arrived at the kitchen window.

"Do come around again," she called over Angie's shoulder, and we all, obnoxious Big Tom included, assured her we would call the next evening.

"You do, and you die!" hissed Big Tom when Simcha was out of sight.

"Yeah?" snarled Subway Pete. "Just try to stop us!"

A dark fur ridge crept along our backs as Big Tom inched menacingly toward Subway Pete. I hissed explosively, "You touch one hair on his body and I'll tear your eyes out!"

"Yeah," threatened Subway Pete, "and you touch one o' my buddy's whiskers and I'll rip off your head!"

"Eeyowrrrr," wailed Big Tom mockingly, as his glistening yellow eyes narrowed into evil slits. "Real tough hey? Just wait 'till I get one o' you alone. We'll see how tough you are then! And I'll get you – I'll get the both of you. Just wait and see."

We refused to be bullied and stood our ground in stiff-legged rage, hissing and growling in his face. Big Tom backed off gradually, muttering and cursing revenge. He finally stalked off in furious defeat. Big Tom knew better than to start a yowling cat fight at Simcha's door. Besides, all of us feared Mrs. Wilkes's broom.

Chapter Nine

It was too early to bed down for the night, so Subway Pete suggested, "Let's mosey on down to the park and see what kind of excitement we can scare up. Yonge Street nightlife can be mighty colorful. You get some real crazies down at the park sometimes, especially on weekends."

We stopped to sharpen our claws on a tree trunk and hopped onto our favorite bench for our evening wash-up. Subway Pete continued, "Miss Calico says it's ten times worse in downtown Toronto – a real jungle. Noisier 'n all get-out in the summer. It's no place to be in winter though, let me tell you. Strays down there will kill for a scrap of food."

A few young couples and a middle-aged man were in the park. The man was walking a big dog, and as they drew near our bench, we crouched tensely, ready to spring to safety. Much to our amusement, the dog started pulling back on his leash when he saw us, his eyes rolling nervously in his head. We waited to see what would happen as the owner tugged at the leash, trying to coax the sandy-colored dog along the walk. The dog would take a few steps, then sit, his big brown eyes darting from our bench to his owner's face.

"Get a look at that, will ya'?" sneered Subway Pete. "That thing's scared silly of cats! Hey pooch—you take one more step and we'll have your hide!"

The dog whimpered and hung back even more firmly on the leash but his annoyed owner persisted in dragging him along. Subway Pete and I stood up, arching our backs and hissing just for the fun of it as the owner dragged the dog past.

Suddenly the man decided to sit down on our bench. His poor dog backed off as far as his leash would allow him, rolling his eyes in fear. We looked over the owner and were not impressed by his appearance or his odor. There was an unnatural glaze to his eyes and his long hair was straggly and matted. He wore a beaded headband and a metallic peace-symbol around his neck. His jeans and T-shirt were in need of laundering and he could have done with a new pair of sandals. One badly worn sandal had a broken ankle strap and the shoe flopped on the pavement with each step.

The man stared right back at us and then surprised us by stating, "You makin' fun o' my buddy here? Huh? He's a scared little animal. You'd be scared too if you'd been beaten and kicked around all yer life! If I hadn't up and rescued him he'd be dead by now."

Subway Pete and I stared at each other in surprise. We

were used to people talking to us, but this man quite clearly seemed to expect us to understand.

He ignored us for a moment and rolled a cigarette that gave off a sweetish odor as he lit it. The man looked at us again. "He don't like people – ya know what I mean? Him and me – we both don't like people, but ya' gotta make the best of it."

He turned to the dog whose eyes rolled pathetically up at him as he spoke. "It's a rotten world, dog, but we gotta keep on livin' and makin' do somehow. You and I can do it."

He turned to us again. "Him and me's been hurt by people, yeah we been hurt bad, but ya can't let it ruin ya. I almost did that, ya know? I almost let it ruin me. This here dog – he's gotta learn that everyone ain't bad. There's a few people you can trust. I'm gonna teach him to trust me and maybe then he can get over his scaredness. Start makin' a few human friends."

He spoke to the dog again, "Hey dog? You don't need to be scared. Why you actin' scared now, huh? These two cats scarin' you?"

The dog whimpered, looking dolefully into his master's face. Again the man stared intently at us. "He's scared a' youse, ain't he? It don't make sense, a dog being scared of cats but that's how he is. I wonder what Joe done to him to make him scared of cats? You two better run along, okay? Hope youse don't mind."

Subway Pete looked at me and I nodded, whereupon we both leapt to the ground and strolled casually on our way.

"If that pooch acts like that around cats, I'd hate to see how he is around people," I muttered.

"And I'd hate to think what kind of life he's had before," added Subway Pete. "Sounds even worse than Timid Gray."

We padded silently along the sidewalk, thinking about

our encounter with the weird dog. Suddenly I was struck by a curious thought and I asked Subway Pete, "Did Nasty Joe ever have a dog?"

"Gee willickers, I don't know? Why do you ask?"

"The guy mentioned something about Joe, remember?"

"Oh yeah – it was something about Joe makin' him scared o' cats. Yeah, I was wondering about that."

"You don't think . . . ?"

"Nah, probably just a coincidence. Maybe someone from the gang would know. You wanna drop by Harry's and see what's cookin'? Maybe you can find something out from Timid Gray. She might remember if there was a dog around."

"Too bad that guy chased us off. We could've asked the dog."

"That thing's too scared to open his yap. I doubt you would have got anything out of him anyway."

We arrived back at the old hangout to find everyone but Miss Calico present. The two of us hopped onto the abandoned freezer and settled down with paws tucked under our chest. We perked our ears attentively as our friends discussed the latest cat events. I smiled as they argued about some of the latest human theories on cat behavior. Doc Jones was sitting like a dignified little senator on the porch steps. When it was his turn to speak up, he stretched himself to full height and began to lecture in an authoritative voice.

"Let me tell you right now," he stated confidently. "Humans for the most part are badly educated about cat behavior. We cats are wonderfully and marvelously created. Even something as simple as a cat's whiskers are a scientific marvel."

There was a mock round of ahhs and rowrrs from the cats but our self-styled professor was not put off by our heckling. He puffed up his chest even more and proceeded with his scholarly lecture. "Technically, whiskers are called vibrissae. They are not just feelers—they are air current detectors. Now you think about that, my fellow cats. Do you realize, as we manoeuvre our way about in the dark that each solid object we approach causes minute disturbances in the air currents? And did you know that our whiskers are so highly sensitized that they can read these air changes and detect the presence of solid obstacles even without touching them!"

Then he concluded, "So you see, my dear companions, I know from whence I speak when I say that we have been marvelously and wondrously created."

The entire group broke out into a cat-calling round of amused applause at which Doc Jones bowed his head, smiled graciously and sat down to allow the next speaker an opportunity to air his views.

Preacher Ted was the next to speak up. "Yes, we are indeed fearfully and wondrously made! And we are created for a noble purpose, my friends. This ol' world is a better place for humankind 'cause o' us cats bein' part of it."

"Preach it, brother! Preach it!" croaked Ugly Ben.

"Now ah asks you friends, what is more satisfying than a cat purrin' contentedly by the fireplace or curled up on his master's lap? How many lonely souls has found comfort in the lovin' company of a friendly cat and how many persons has done turned to cats for solace in a world full a' frettin' and fussin'?"

The gang purred and meowed approval. Preacher Ted sat down, smiled modestly and licked his nose self-consciously.

"Right on," added Truckin' Sam. "Does a cat care if his home is an untidy one-room shack or a spotless mansion? There's no strings attached to a cat's loving, 'ceptin' for a decent meal and a bit of kindness, and what's that in comparison to the joy and satisfaction we bring them?"

"My, my, my," sneered Ugly Ben. "Ain't we a saintly bunch."

"Well now, Ugly Ben," said Pretty Sal, "a cat's gotta do what a cat's gotta do. I think most cat-loving persons are willing to overlook a few of our minor faults in return for the pleasure of our company."

"Hear! Hear!" called out several cats.

Suddenly, without warning, Miss Calico came flying into our midst with her fur still bristling. She leaped onto the porch and paced anxiously back and forth as she explained breathlessly, "Oh my . . . I've just had an awful fright! You can't imagine what that dreadful Nasty Joe is up to now!"

She paused for effect and gazed around the circle of cats that sat like frozen statues waiting for her to continue. "He's taken to cruising up and down the side streets on the hunt for strays and he's got a big net . . . oh it's ghastly. One moment you're snoozing peacefully on a window sill and the next moment that . . . that monster is creeping up on you with a net in his hands and the wickedest look on his face."

"This calls for war, boys and girls!" growled Ugly Ben. "Those yard traps were bad enough, but now he's gone too far. If he's not stopped soon there won't be a cat left alive on the streets of Rosedale."

Angry yowling and debating went on that night as we argued about what should be done to put a stop to Nasty Joe's murderous rampage. We might even have come to some sort of plan if several irate people had not shouted at us to be quiet and thrown some objects to frighten us off. That night, safely nestled in the toolshed, Subway Pete and I vowed that we would end Nasty Joe's rampages if it was the last thing we ever did!

Chapter Ten

The next afternoon brought a surprising discovery. We were lying on Cindy's patio, sunning ourselves and talking about the events of the night before. When we described what had happened in the park with the dog, Cindy jumped to her feet and exclaimed, "Was he a sandy-colored dog with big, brown eyes?"

"Why yes, he was," I replied.

"And you say he'd been very badly treated by somebody?"

"It appeared that way. In fact, Joe's name was mentioned but we thought . . . ."

"Why, then it must be!" she interrupted. Cindy looked as though she had just sighted a quail for she stood poised bird-dog fashion with her head forward, one paw uplifted and tail fanned out like a hunting dog in action. We could not help but smile in amusement and when she realized how funny she looked she plopped down on her hind end, shaking her head slowly as she spoke. "Well, I'll be. Now isn't that a coincidence!"

The pups stopped their tumbling and tussling to stare curiously at their mother and each other.

"What is it, Ma? What's happening?"

"It's Hank, children. I'm sure it's Hank. He disappeared about a week ago. You remember Hank?"

The children's eyes were bright and round.

"Yeah, sure!" they exclaimed. Duffy then informed us that poor Hank would have starved to death if they hadn't allowed him to come sneaking over for some dog food now and again.

"I never thought to mention it to you when we were talking about Nasty Joe the other day," said Cindy. "Hank used to belong to Nasty Joe! Oh, I'm so glad he's been adopted by a caring person. The Humane Society would never have been able to place him. He was hopelessly maladjusted!"

"True," said Subway Pete, "but his new owner was just as bad. I guess the poor hound can't be choosy. It sounds like the guy knew Nasty Joe. At least it seemed that way from the way he was talking."

"Hey Ma," exclaimed one of the pups, "that man shoulda turned Nasty Joe in to the police, that's what he shoulda done, huh!"

"Yeah," chorused the others as they bounded around their mother.

Cindy looked very thoughtful. "It's too bad Mark and Helen never met poor, skinny Hank but he always took off when they came around. I'm sure they would have gotten after Nasty Joe if they had known he was mistreating Hank. They made him get rid of his traps, you know."

"Oh!" I cried. "So that's why he's cruising the streets in the old van and using a net to chase us down!"

"You're kidding!" Cindy responded.

We kid you not!" declared Subway Pete."You better warn your adopted strays to stay close to home. I don't think Nasty Joe knows or cares whether or not a cat is a stray," cautioned Subway Pete.

"Did Hank say much about Nasty Joe?" I asked.

"Not really. Usually he'd just gobble his food and run. I could see he was mistreated. And yes, now that I remember, he did avoid the cats. I wonder if we could get hold of him somehow. He probably knows where Nasty Joe keeps his gun. He just might be a help to us."

"We'll keep an eye out for him in the park," said Subway Pete. "He probably lives in the area."

"Oh yes, do that," Cindy replied eagerly. "I'll ask around and try to find out where he's living. Maybe I could lead Mark and Helen to his new owner."

"Hey Ma," yelped a wriggly pup, "is Hank's master gonna help us put Nasty Joe in jail?"

"Oh wow, neat!" squealed another pup.

"Yay and good riddance to bad rubbish," cried a third.

The pups leaped and pranced around, insulting Nasty Joe.

"Somehow Mark and Helen must establish contact with Hank's new owner," said Cindy. "They're pretty annoyed with Nasty Joe right now. They intend to find out what he was doing with the animals he was trapping in those cages.

Hank's new owner might be able to give them a few clues in their investigation."

"Right on," replied Subway Pete, "and it's a good bet that Hank's owner would like to see old Nasty Joe get his ears pinned back."

"Nasty Joe's a mean old crow," chanted one of the pups."

"Nasty Joe has gotta go," chanted another.

"Now stop!" scolded their mother. "I'll not have any more name-calling."

The pups continued to frolic and leap, but nothing more was said about Nasty Joe. I admired how well they obeyed their mother.

The strays joined us for lunch and remained to spend the afternoon in pleasant conversation. We left Cindy with her pups curled peacefully by her side.

As we made our way to Angie's place, we met Ugly Ben sitting on a park bench. The news about Nasty Joe prowling the streets with his van had upset him greatly and he was very depressed. He grumbled when we tried to cheer him up.

"Grrmph," muttered Ugly Ben, "you're still a couple of fleet-footed youngsters. It's us crippled oldsters that gotta worry. My days are numbered. I can feel it in my bones. I'll be mighty lucky if I make it through another winter."

We both began talking at once, trying to reassure and encourage him but he ignored us, shook his head sadly and laid his head on his paws, then slowly closed his eyes for a nap. Subway Pete and I left in a subdued mood. Had our minds not been so distracted over Ugly Ben's plight we would have noticed that we were being stalked by Big Tom!

We trotted lazily across lawns and along back lanes as Big Tom gained steadily on us. By the time we caught his scent, he was almost on top of us. We swung around to face him just as he lunged into view from behind a parked car.

Even now, as I recall that unforgettable scene, I can feel the fur on my back rising. Spitting, snarling and shrieking wildly we flew into a swirling tangle of flying fur and lashing claws. Sometimes Subway Pete or I would be momentarily clawed or kicked out of the huddle but we always dove right back in, biting and clawing furiously at our tormentor as we fought. Subway Pete yelled at me to run but I had no intention of leaving him to face Big Tom's murderous rage alone. At times we stopped, spitting and hissing as we withdrew a few paces to circle around and reposition ourselves for renewed attacks. Then we leaped back into battle, piercing the air with screams of rage and anger as flashing claws, flying feet, tails and tufts of fur swirled madly round and round.

Several times I winced from the pain of Big Tom's sharp claws ripping across my face and along my back. Twice his teeth tore into my body, once above my shoulder, dangerously close to my neck and another time he ripped savagely into my left ear. Finally, half-blinded by the salty blood that ran from my face wounds and torn ear, I staggered off to one side, panting and gasping for breath. Fortunately for both of us, Big Tom had enough as well. He let out another enraged howl as Subway Pete sank his teeth into his neck. He yanked himself loose, turned and ran. We yowled insults after him until he was out of sight, then limped over to a grassy yard so we could clean our wounds and rest.

As we crawled into the shade of a small shrub, Subway Pete looked at me and wailed mournfully, "Why'd ya do it, buddy? You're a ruined cat!! I'll never forgive myself. You shoulda' done like I told ya' and run off. I'da managed on my own."

"No way," I replied stubbornly. "He'd of killed you."

For the next while neither of us spoke as we licked and cleaned painful wounds and filthy fur. It was not an easy task.

Some of my wounds were difficult to reach but I licked gingerly at what I could reach, then cleaned carefully with a dampened paw, trying to ignore the searing pain. I did not even try to clean my ear, for the slightest touch set off a piercing pain. I smiled ruefully as I realized that torn ear was my initiation into the world of strays. I was no longer a temporary visitor – I was now a part of the gang. I was truly one of them. Even if Penners were to find me, there would be no trophies or blue ribbons or adoring crowds and flashing cameras. As I realized that I was indeed a "ruined cat," I felt overcome with despair. Had it not been for Subway Pete, I know I would have wailed pitifully. Instead, I tried to keep up a brave front. How I longed to curl up by my mother's side like a tiny kitten. I longed for her wise and reassuring words and the comfort of her love. I wondered what my beautiful Grand Champion father would have said to his scarred and disfigured son. I sighed as I told Subway Pete that I really did not care to visit Simcha that night.

"She'll be shocked; she'll pity me," I whimpered mournfully. "She already feels sorry for me. I really can't face her. In fact, I don't ever want to go back there again."

"Hogwash," he scolded. "You're going there tonight!"

"But I can't!" I protested.

"Hey boy – what is this Simcha chick? A true lady or an unfeeling snob?"

"Now wait a minute . . . I. . . he's . . . ."

"I win!" he proclaimed with his endearing, lopsided grin. "Let's go!"

When Angie unlatched the front gate and saw our battle wounds she almost dropped Simcha. "Oh Simcha, look at them!" she gasped. "Some huge dog must have been after them. Oh, the poor darlings. We've got to help them."

She set Simcha on the ground and beckoned us to follow her down the walkway and into the house.

"No way," Subway Pete protested. "I wouldn't go near that dragon lady for love or money."

"Oh, stop your fussing," ordered Simcha. "You're both in a dreadful state and you need to get some antiseptic on those wounds."

"But what if she turns us over to Animal Control?" he asked.

Simcha scolded gently, "Listen, Angie wouldn't stand for anything like that, neither would Mr. Wilkes. Trust me a bit, why don't you?"

I proceeded to follow Angie and Simcha to the house. Subway Pete followed meekly behind and in no time we were standing inside the forbidden, beautiful Wilkes's estate!

Chapter Eleven

Mrs. Wilkes was not pleased!

"Angie!" she scolded. "What on earth are you doing bringing those disease-ridden creatures in here. Good grief, look at them! They're a mess! Your carelessness will be the death of Simcha yet."

Mrs. Wilkes's voice grew louder. "I have warned you repeatedly that purebred showcats must never be exposed to potential disease sources. You know what great care and expense we take to keep her environment sterile!"

"Yeah," snapped Angie, "sterile is the word for it, and I'm sick of it. So is Simcha. When I grow up, I'm going to have a dozen cats in my house and they're all gonna be strays!"

"Angie! Whatever has gotten into you?" she gasped. "Wait until your father hears. . ."

"Aw Mom, c'mon. Look at the poor things! How could I just leave them to wander the streets like that, suffering and maybe dying from infections? What the heck, aren't cats like these the reason for our charity shows? C'mon Mum, we can't be hypocrites. We gotta practice what we're preaching."

The Dragon smiled grudgingly and looked at us somewhat more tolerantly. Subway Pete and I sat motionless as the formidable Mrs. Wilkes studied us, frowning thoughtfully. We were silent in her presence and awestruck at our luxurious new surroundings. The chandelier with its myriad, rainbow reflections glimmered enchantingly and the long, winding oak staircase beckoned me to climb and explore.

Mrs. Wilkes's frown grew more concentrated as she examined me. Then she remarked, "I doubt the Siamese is a stray. His owners are going to be heartsick about the mess he's gotten himself into. That ear needs surgical attention. We must try to find his people. Perhaps we can find a home for the other cat as well. Meanwhile, get Odette to help clean them up and tend their scrapes."

Mrs. Wilkes picked Simcha up and smiled for the first time. "We shall have to keep Simcha shut in the trophy room for now. It would be intolerable if she were to pick up fleas or infection from those poor creatures."

Simcha smiled mischievously over Mrs. Wilkes's shoulder and teased, "Wait'll Odette finds out you have fleas – rowrrr!"

"Oh no," muttered Subway Pete. "You ever had a flea bath?"

"No," I replied fearfully, "but I hear they're horrendous."

"Maybe we oughta' run for it!"

"It's that bad?"

"Uh huh. But on second thought, maybe we better stay cool, kid. This place is luxury city—let's not spoil a good thing. If it means me getting adopted and you finding your family, it'll be worth a bit of suffering."

"Yes, that would be great, you finding a home, but I wonder what Penners will think. The main reason they kept me was because they figured I was going to be a Grand Champion showstar some day. Now they probably couldn't even give me away!"

Subway Pete opened his mouth to reply but Odette appeared to help Angie carry us up the winding stairway to an extremely large bathroom. They set us on soft mats on either side of the sink and I glanced in the mirror and stared mournfully at my battered face and torn ear. One eye was swollen and part of the torn ear flopped over pathetically. I was more sure than ever that the Penners would no longer want me and wondered whatever would become of me. My heart sank as the maid began running the bath water.

"How does she know if we have fleas?" I asked.

"I hate being stereotyped," Subway Pete grumbled indignantly.

"What's stereotyped?" I asked.

"It's like when people say all Siamese are temperamental. These kind of people think all strays are dirty, diseased and flea-ridden."

"Oh!"

Odette opened a cupboard beneath the sink and brought out a tray of salves and medicinal supplies, then opened a drawer and took out an armful of towels and another thick, soft mat for us to sit on while being toweled dry. I shivered nervously and Angie stroked me and spoke soothingly. "It's all right, darlings. I shall be very gentle. Oh, how I wish I could keep you for my own."

"We shall put them in your room until they're dry," said Odette. "Now don't get attached to them because it'll make giving them up even more difficult."

Angie was very gentle as she promised, but it was still most upsetting to be doused with strange chemicals and plunged into a tub full of water. While I was being bathed, I yowled as much from nervousness as from pain, and poor Subway Pete scrambled off the counter and hid behind the toilet, grumbling and muttering in disgust. "Quit yer belly-achin'. You're unnerving me," he complained.

"You'll yell too when that flea shampoo gets into your cuts," I replied with a snarl.

"Thanks, pal. You sure know how to reassure a guy."

Odette toweled me dry while Angie bathed Subway Pete. He fussed even more than I did but Angie praised us anyway for being good. At least we did not attempt to scratch or bite her. I hated the obnoxious medicinal smells and squirmed from the stinging disinfectant.

"This is awful," I whined.

"Hang in there, kid. Won't be long now. Man, are we gonna have a blast casing this place out. I wonder if we'll be allowed to associate with Lady Simcha?"

"Where there's a will, there's a way," I replied.

"Right on! You're a cat after my own heart," he joked.

"Wait till we tell the gang about this," I exclaimed. "Do you think Mrs. Wilkes will let us outside?"

"That's hard to say. We're not fancy showcats, I don't see why we shouldn't be free to come and go."

I sighed and Subway Pete apologized. "Gee kid, I'm sorry. I forgot . . . "

"It's okay. I gotta face the facts. I'm all washed up as a showcat – get the pun? All washed up! Ha, ha."

Subway Pete just looked at me sadly.

Angie and Odette bundled us into the soft towels and carried us to Angie's room. I hated being trapped in the towel and struggled to escape but gave up from the pain it caused. Angie's room was full of clean fresh fragrances. I was eager to inspect the interesting new odors, but first I wanted to clean all the hateful medicinal smells from my body and restore my own odor.

The moment we were free of the towels, we scurried to a place where we could hide and calm down before cleaning up. Subway Pete scrambled under the bed and I crawled under a chair.

Angie lingered at the door and spoke kindly. "I'll leave you alone for a little while, okay? Just make yourselves at home and I'll bring you some special treats later. I can hardly wait for you to meet Dad. He'll love you too."

I stayed under my chair for awhile after the door closed, then crept slowly out into the open.

Subway Pete popped his head out from under the bed and grinned. "Coast clear?"

"Yup. There's special goodies coming later – and look at that soft bed; those big fluffy pillows!"

"Wowrr, what a setup," he proclaimed as he crawled from under the bed.

"What was Truckin' Sam saying about cats not caring if their home was a mansion or a shack?" I teased.

"Now hold on a minute. Us cats do like the finer things in life but if we can't have them we're no less happy. It's too bad people aren't that way."

"What makes you think they aren't?"

Subway Pete grinned. "Can you imagine the Dragon being happy in a dirty, flea-infested, one-room hovel?"

"No, but you'd fit right in!"

Subway Pete swatted playfully at me and I hopped out of reach.

We cleaned our coats vigorously, grumbling occasionally about the repulsive odors. Even after a thorough wash down, some scent lingered but Subway Pete assured me it would disappear in a few days. We investigated the room, then jumped on the bed to rest.

I was very exhausted and slept soundly until Angie brought our bedtime snack. She sat by our side watching us eat, talking to us about her friends and school and summer holiday plans as she stroked our fur. She cuddled us when we were finished our meal, buried her nose in our fur and told us we smelled "beautiful."

"She's just saying that to make us feel good," I said. "She can't mean it."

"People have many strange quirks, my boy. She probably does like the way we smell."

"I'm going to put off finding homes for you as long as I can," she informed us. "If I can get Dad to fall in love with you too, maybe he can talk Mom into letting me keep you. You must help me though. You have to be on your best behavior and stay out of mischief. No knocking over the plants or getting in Odette's way or pestering the cockatiels."

"Cockatiels?" I asked. "What are cockatiels?"

"Beats me," responded Subway Pete. "I hope they aren't dogs."

"And no clawing the furniture," she added, "or Mum will whack you with the broom."

"Hmph," muttered Subway Pete. "I'm not so sure if this place really is my style."

"Oh c'mon, give it a couple days," I coaxed. "You're the one that's always looking for adventure. Well, this is adventure if ever there was adventure."

"True, true," he admitted. "I don't suppose it would hurt me to learn a bit of class. I just hope that cockatiels aren't something tasty like mice."

"It'd do us good to learn to resist temptation too," I teased.

That evening Angie's father came to visit us and as he entered the room, Subway Pete joked, "Now there is a beautiful smell."

"Right on," I added. "Those Harry's Diner fragrances are heaven on earth."

Mr. Wilkes recognized me from my visits to the diner and laughed. "You sure get around, don't you, little man? I better pop you off at the vet's on my way to work tomorrow. That ear needs a patch-up job."

Mr. Wilkes picked me up and scratched under my chin. We love that sort of thing and I rewarded him by purring happily. Angie cradled Subway Pete in her arms and smiled winsomely at her father.

We curled up on Angie's bed after Mr. Wilkes was gone and settled down for another nap while Angie played a computer game. Subway Pete was still sleeping when I awoke and Angie was absorbed in her game. I hopped off the bed, moved soundlessly through the open doorway and crept along the hall landing to the staircase. I stopped at the top and sat down to inspect and scent my surroundings before moving on.

The big house was very still and I quivered excitedly as I drifted soundlessly down the richly carpeted steps. The living room was enormous and it took a good twenty minutes to explore it fully. I heard someone walking around in another room and hid behind the couch until everything was silent again. I sniffed about the dining room, filled with a lovely natural wood fragrance from the huge oak dining room suite. Then I wandered into the spacious kitchen with its pleasant food and spice odors. Suddenly I caught a distinctively bird-like odor and stopped still in my tracks.

"Eeyikes! Wake up Cyrano! There's a strange cat in the house!"

I crouched to the floor as my gaze darted to a large bird cage that was suspended from the ceiling in a little sun room alcove off the main kitchen area.

"Yeah, ya little jerk, we're right over here, safely out of reach. How the dickens did you get inside the house?"

I sat speechless. It was not the first time I'd been told off by a bird, but it was my first encounter with caged birds.

I continued to stare stupidly as both of the parrot-like birds sidled along their perch to stare down at me. One was mostly gray with white feathers bordering the shoulder edge of his wings. He had a bright circular orange cheek patch on each side of his yellow face. The female was a snowy-white with the same yellow head and bright orange cheek patches as her mate. Both had tufted yellow plumes on their heads, giving them a distinguished look. It suddenly dawned on me that these were the cockatiels Angie had warned us not to bother.

The gray bird was even more insulting than his white mate. "Flake off, ya little creep," he warned.

This made me angry. I hissed at them and walked right up to the cage, then sat glaring furiously as my tail twitched back and forth.

"You must forgive my new houseguest," said a gentle voice behind my back. "He is a wee bit lacking in some of the social graces."

I spun around to find Simcha sitting in the kitchen doorway, her eyes shining with mischief.

Simcha introduced me politely. "Shalom, these birds are my good friends, Cyrano and Precious." She waited quietly for me to respond but I simply could not bring myself to say "how do you do" or "pleased to meet you."

Instead I replied snidely, "Spare me the introductions, please. They are two of the rudest little twits I have ever met."

The birds eyed me sharply with their bright, intelligent black eyes as Simcha explained, "It's only because they are frightened. They are really delightfully witty and sociable."

"Oh yes, quite true, quite true," chirped Cyrano. "We had no idea you were a proper guest and you did sneak up on us quite unexpectedly."

"You—you're friends with them?" I asked Simcha in amazement.

"We get along very well, thank you," added Precious.

"Oh yeah?" I replied skeptically. "Then why are you locked up in a cage way off the ground?"

"Oh, we're often let out to roam during the day," said Precious, "but you can rest assured that won't happen while you're around!"

"How long ya staying, blue eyes?" asked Cyrano.

"And what happened to your face?" asked Precious.

"It was Big Tom, wasn't it," asked Simcha. "I scented his odor all over both of you. You may be very sure he'll never set foot on our property again!"

I sighed and looked sadly down at the floor.

"Shalom?" she asked quietly. "Why didn't you just run?"

"I. . .he caught us unaware."

"Why? Why did he go after you?" she asked angrily.

I shuffled uneasily, still looking at the ground, and Precious spoke up, admonishing Simcha. "Hey, wake up and smell the coffee. Old Big Tom's jealous of Mr. Blue Eyes. He doesn't want any competition."

"Lookit the poor fellow," taunted Cyrano. "He's head-over-heels in love with you!"

I glared at Precious and Cyrano, miserable with embarrassment.

"Ah yes," Simcha replied softly. "I should have realized . . ."

I looked up at Simcha and responded angrily, "Do you pity me now, because I'm no longer destined for blue ribbons and cheering crowds? Perhaps the Penners will keep me out of pity but I have ruined all the dreams they had for me. And my parents – how can I face them?"

Simcha's fathomless blue eyes gazed unwaveringly into mine. We sat facing each other silently and my anger began to fade as I saw the concern in her eyes. She replied quietly, "Was it not you who once said that my mistress needed to learn that a cat doesn't have to have a fancy pedigree to be something special? Does one need to be a great success or star to find happiness? Aren't some of the finest cats you've met strays like Subway Pete and his gang? The creature to be pitied is the one who loves only himself."

We sat for a long while again, looking into each other's eyes. At last I smiled and Simcha's enchanting blue eyes glowed happily. The birds chirped and twittered, siddling back and forth along their perch but we took no notice of them as we sat and chatted. At the sound of Mrs. Wilkes's footsteps, Simcha winked and darted off to her room while I scurried back to Angie's bedroom.

Chapter Twelve

Mr. Wilkes dropped me off at the vet's for surgery in the morning and I awoke from the anesthetic about mid-day, feeling so dizzy I could hardly hold up my head. I put my head down on my paws, but the whole room continued to sway and reel. It was no use trying to look around for my eyes could hardly focus. I lay still, eyes closed, waiting for the nauseous feeling and dizziness to subside. My ear throbbed slightly but was really not too painful. I was glad it was over and done.

A vet came in to tend the other animals, then checked my cage. "Wake up, sleepyhead," she coaxed. "Would you like a wee bit of water?"

The water smelled good and my throat felt dry, but I wasn't sure if it would be worth the effort to get up and lap from the dish. The vet seemed to realize how I felt for she tipped the bowl sideways for me and lifted my head a bit to help me lap the water.

When I was able to focus my eyes, I noticed there were only three other cats in at the time. I did not feel much like talking with them. Doc Jones came by during the supper hour. He was very angry to hear how Big Tom had bullied us! I was pleased to learn that Truckin' Sam had tracked down old Hank and informed Cindy of his whereabouts.

"We'll keep you cats posted on the latest happenings," he promised. "Enjoy your life of luxury. The gang's going to be jealous."

"I don't know how long it's going to last," I replied. "Angie wants to adopt us but the Dragon won't hear of it. But she did offer to find Subway Pete a home and she's promised to try to locate my owners, so she's not completely heartless."

Doc Jones sat on the clean tile floor, looking up earnestly as he spoke. "Be great if you could be reunited with your family."

I agreed but did not tell Doc Jones how much I worried about the way the Penners would respond to my battered-up appearance. He did not know they had kept me because of my potential as a showcat. Doc Jones licked a paw as he looked up at me with a twinkle in his eyes. "How are you getting on with Simcha?" he teased.

"Not bad," I said. "She's really quite a decent sort. Not at all snooty."

"Good-looking too, huh? Purrr?"

I just grinned and informed him that famous showcats do not choose their own partners.

"What?" he laughed. "I've heard of humans arranging marriages for each other but this is ridiculous!" Then he grinned roguishly. "She could elope, you know!"

Later that day, Subway Pete and I lay curled on Angie's bed yawning and purring contentedly.

"Feel like going for a bit of a run tonight?" he asked.

"Will they let us out?"

"Sure. I was meowing at the door this afternoon and Odette let me out for a while. You gotta kick up a bit of a racket, that's all. We'll check in on the gang and head back in time for Simcha's walk. And this time we'll keep our ears and noses tuned for Big Tom."

We arrived at Harry's just in time to catch Doc Jones's lecture on cat grooming. He stopped briefly to acknowledge our arrival with a friendly nod, then continued his lecture. "Most cats, as you no doubt realize, engage in a scent-sharing process with humans."

"Only if you like people," muttered Ugly Ben.

"Or aren't scared of them," added Timid Gray.

"Yes yes, of course," apologized Doc Jones. "It was only a general statement. Most cats, however, do engage in scent-sharing with humans. I'm sure you're all aware of the method."

"Give us a demo, Doc," joked Pretty Sal.

"Ahem, well yes, I shall try. You shall have to imagine that I have here, standing beside me, a friendly human."

Doc Jones pretended to rub up against the imaginary human's leg. "We usually begin by pressing against the human with the top of our head or the side of our face, after which we rub all along our flank. Then we twine our tail around his or her legs and give the human an endearing gaze. Sometimes we repeat the process several times. If the human reaches down to stroke us, we persist with the rubbing; push the side of the mouth against his or her hand and nudge affectionately with the top of our head.

"It is important that friendly cats should be scent-sharing in this way. This makes us feel more at home with our human companions. Why, I know of some stray cats who have so charmed a human with this friendly exercise that they were picked up and adopted on the spot." This statement was met with meows of approval and delight. "And so concludes our lecture for tonight," he finished. "Tomorrow night we will discuss why a cat arches its back when it sees a strange dog."

"Yeah," grouched Ugly Ben, "if we survive that long. I noticed Nasty Joe's van parked in one o' those side streets just off Yonge. There's trouble in the air. I think he's mad about Cindy's owners making him ditch the traps, so now he's coming after us with the van."

"By the way," I asked, "has anyone heard anything more about Hank?"

"Sure have," announced Truckin' Sam. "We were talking about it before you came. Cindy was able to reach Hank and spoke to him a bit about the trouble us cats are having with Nasty Joe. Hank says he's sick to death of Nasty Joe and if he ever sees him again he's gonna give him a butt full of teeth!"

This news was greeted with yowls of delight. I looked guiltily at Subway Pete, remembering how we had teased the poor dog.

"Cindy says his new owner's name is Ronald," said Truckin' Sam. "Apparently he's a very kind master and is trying to help Hank get over his fears. He takes Hank for walks at night in the park to help him overcome his fear of people."

"And cats," I added ruefully.

"Yeah," added Truckin' Sam, "he associates cats with his bad memories of those trips to the garbage dump. He says Nasty Joe usually just dumped the cats. There were only a few times he actually shot at them. Hank always knew when Nasty Joe was in a killing mood 'cause there'd be a gun in the van."

There were audible sighs of relief. It was good to know that most of the cats had escaped alive.

"Hank says he hated those trips to the dump," he continued, "but Nasty Joe forced him to go and would kick him if he refused to get in the van."

"Tell them about the drugs," exclaimed Miss Calico.

"Oh yeah, that's another thing," added Truckin' Sam. "Ronald was buying marijuana from Nasty Joe before he stole his dog. Hank says Ronald can't stand cruelty to animals, that's why he stole Hank and became enemies with Nasty Joe."

"Hmm," said Doc Jones. "I wonder if the drugs are what's making Nasty Joe so crazy? Lots of people get mad at us for getting into their garbage and yowling at night, but they aren't rounding up cats for target practice at the garbage dump. I hope Ronald turns old Nasty Joe in to the police for drug-dealing so they can lock him up and throw away the key!"

"Nasty Joe is one friend that Ronald can sure 'nuff do without," said Preacher Ted.

"Amen brother," croaked Ugly Ben. "Nasty Joe is one person the whole world can do without."

"What's marijuana?" I asked.

"It's stuff that some people smoke to make themselves feel high," said Miss Calico.

"High?" I asked.

"Works like catnip," said Doc Jones.

"Owrowrrrr!" chorused several cats.

Miss Calico smiled demurely in our direction and inquired with a coy smile, "How do you two like living in the lap of luxury?"

"Heavenly," purred Subway Pete.

The gang teased us about our good fortune but all, even Ugly Ben, congratulated us most heartily. Mr. Wilkes was busy that night and left our feeding to Carl, who tossed the food out hurriedly without even glancing at us.

Ugly Ben joined us as we headed towards Yonge Street. We sensed that he was lonely and offered to spend some time with him in the park before returning home. He agreed gratefully and walked along, wheezing asthmatically by our side.

We ambled leisurely down the lane toward Yonge and were a short distance from the main street when Subway Pete stopped suddenly, his nose quivering excitedly. A moment later I caught and recognized the scent of Nasty Joe!

"Careful, Ugly Ben," he warned. "It's Nasty Joe."

Ugly Ben sniffed the air nervously, but it took him a while to catch the scent. I felt sorry for him as I realized that all the senses essential to a cat's survival were swiftly failing him. His eyes darted anxiously about and the rasping wheeze grew louder as his breathing became more tense.

We slowed down, peering and sniffing cautiously. "It's strange," said Subway Pete. "He's usually right with the old van. It must be parked around here somewhere, but I can't scent it."

"It's a trick," hissed Ugly Ben. "He's always changing his hunting tactics."

"His scent's getting stronger," I cried. "We better hightail it back the way we came!"

Before my friends had a chance to respond, Nasty Joe darted out from between two buildings and lunged toward us waving a large net in his hands!

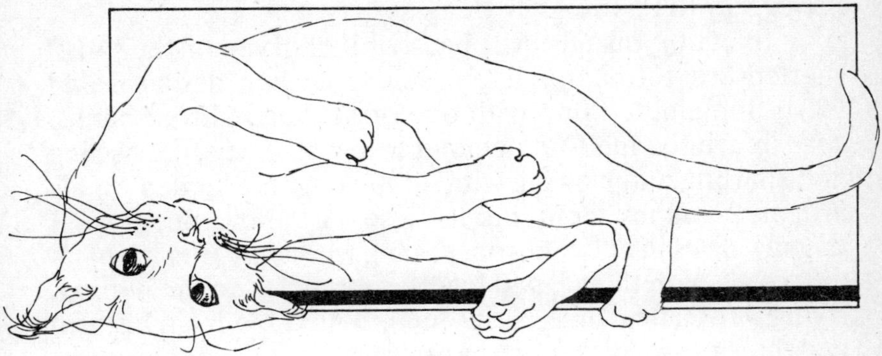

Chapter Thirteen

"Run!" yowled Subway Pete as he tore past Nasty Joe and bolted toward Yonge Street, yelling at us to head for the park.

We began to run but Nasty Joe leaped into the middle of the alley and blocked our path. We crouched, staring at our wild-eyed enemy. In the partial darkness he loomed ominously larger. His hands and arms seemed monstrous. Later I realized it was because he was wearing thick elbow-length leather gloves. He crouched menacingly, muttered unintelligibly, then swung a large iron-framed net at us. I could hear the net whipping through the air and landing with a solid THUMP! right over the cowering Ugly Ben. His yowls were so incredibly loud I could hardly believe my ears. He struggled so hard and furiously I was afraid he would kill himself. I hesitated, torn between the desire to save my own life or stay to rescue Ugly Ben.

"Shut up, you ugly little beast or I'll kill you on the spot!" snarled our tormentor. Ugly Ben screeched defiance and Nasty Joe clouted him with one of his huge gloved hands. This infuriated me so much that I flew at Nasty Joe, hissing and snarling and clawing with all my might. I landed on his arm and sank my teeth into its flesh, just above the glove. I dug my claws in and hung on, joining with Ugly Ben in snarls and yowls of defiant fury. Ugly Ben struggled in the netting, trying to escape, while Nasty Joe grabbed me from his arm and flung me so hard against a brick wall that I lost consciousness.

As I began to revive, I could hear Ugly Ben's voice, croakier then ever. "Shalom? Shalom, are you still alive?"

I shook my head dazedly and tried to get off the ground but my hind legs seemed paralyzed. I could not struggle to my feet no matter how hard I tried. I collapsed, shivering with fright and pain, sickened by the strong odors of Nasty Joe that seemed to fill the air. I was conscious of angry human voices and a barking dog nearby, intermingled with Yonge Street traffic sounds, but I couldn't understand where we were and peered into the semidarkness, trying desperately to focus. I felt even more helpless when I realized that we were both penned inside cages.

"We're doomed, my friend," whimpered Ugly Ben. "He's trapped us in his van, threatening to kill us both. You're a fool, kid. You shoulda' run when you had a chance. I'm old – it doesn't matter – but you . . . "

I groaned in pain and despair and lay my head on my paws, too discouraged to even try to speak. Poor Ugly Ben was wheezing and gasping as though on his deathbed.

The noise and commotion outside the van increased. We perked our ears to catch what was going on. The angry voices and barking dog were directly beside our van now and someone was yelling, "Police! Police! Mad dog!"

"He ain't no mad dog!" yelled another man and I recognized the voice immediately.

"It's . . . it's Ronald!" I shouted. "That must be Hank with him!"

Suddenly the van shuddered as something banged against its side.

"Call him off!" shrieked Nasty Joe.

"No way. pal! He's got a score to settle. . . ." Then there was more yelling and barking and commotion with people hollering for the police.

"Ugly Ben, there's hope!" I cried. "If we yowl like mad maybe. . . ."

The van shuddered again as the fighting outside continued and in the distance we detected the faint wailing of a police siren.

Ugly Ben and I set up such a yowling and caterwauling that someone shouted, "What the devil was that?"

We kept up our howling and moaning until someone yanked the van's back doors wide open. The sight of those friendly, concerned faces filled me with pure happiness. Ugly Ben licked his nose nervously and I purred! It seems impossible that a cat would purr in the midst of all that pain and fright but that's exactly what I did. If I could have stood up I would have rubbed against the cage in friendly greeting.

When the police stepped out of their squad cars there was more commotion as they arrested Nasty Joe and Ronald.

I heard one of the police instructing the crowd to stay clear of the dog.

"He ain't no rabid hound!" shouted Ronald. "He was. . . ."

"Settle down," replied an officer. "The Humane Society's van is on the way. No one's going to hurt the mutt, now move it."

Ronald and Nasty Joe hollered and yelled at each other as they were shoved into separate squad cars.

Finally a police officer pushed his way through the crowd to peer inside the van. He stared in surprise as we meowed a grateful welcome. "Poor little beggars. Wonder what he was planning to do with you?" He disappeared momentarily. We could hear Hank whimpering and howling outside.

Suddenly a familiar face appeared amongst those gazing into the van. I meowed eagerly for it was Harry Wilkes himself! He stared intently and then demanded, "For crying out loud, what are you doing here?"

I meowed joyously and tried to stand but sank weakly to the floor.

The police officer elbowed his way into the crowd again and ordered them to "move along."

"That's my cat!" Mr. Wilkes called out.

"You sure?" asked the officer.

"Positive! Look at his ear. We had that done just this morning."

"Yeah? Well, you can sort it out with the fellows from the Humane Society, but these animals have to be impounded first. You'll have to move along now, I must inspect this vehicle."

The officer climbed in with a flashlight. Ugly Ben cowered nervously until the policeman reassured him, "Calm down, old man, no one's going to hurt you. Just here for a quick look around, okay?"

Ugly Ben settled down again, keeping a wary eye on the officer. Suddenly the flashlight beam froze in one spot and the officer frowned as he leaned over to inspect more closely. He picked up a gun and without another glance in our direction headed back to his car.

"Nasty Joe's cooked his goose," chortled Ugly Ben. "They'll get him for animal abuse for sure now. Probably get him for drugs as well."

"Yeah. I hope that Ronald character squeals on him. And I hope old Hank took a good chunk out of him."

"Serves him right."

We were silent, listening to the excited voices and Hank's whimpering. Then Ugly Ben spoke again. "You know what that gun meant, don't you, young feller?"

"Yeah, he'd 'of blinked us out for sure."

"But they caught him red-handed."

"Yup! Red-handed."

"Well, as Preacher Ted would probably say, the Lord moves in mysterious ways. . . ."

I smiled in spite of my pain.

We watched a white vehicle with an orange flashing light drive by. I guessed it to be the Humane Society's ambulance and waited nervously to see what would happen next. The van drove ahead and stopped, then backed up slowly to our van. We were loaded, cages and all, into the vehicle along with a very dispirited Hank. Because the trembling dog crouched into the corner of his cage, we could hardly believe it was the same bundle of fury that had attacked Nasty Joe. He whimpered pitifully, rolling his eyes as the van doors clanged shut like a heavy prison gate. I wanted to reassure him that our owners would soon be around to pick us up, but checked myself just in time. There would be no caring owner to rescue the unfortunate Ugly Ben. I whined mournfully.

Hank quit his whimpering and turned his doleful brown eyes on me. "Uh – about your pal, Subway Pete . . . " he began. We were instantly alert, perking our ears forward to learn what had become of Subway Pete. Hank continued, "He was running through the park and yelling that Nasty Joe was after him . . . I. . . ."

The dog hesitated and I asked anxiously, "Was he . . . did Nasty Joe get him?"

"No."

"C'mon pal, tell us what happened," Ugly Ben cried.

"Last I saw he was pushing under the fence by them tracks. I guess he's hiding out in the ravine. Hope he's okay. We could see Joe's van from the park and we saw Joe coming out of the alley with you fellows and dumping you in the van. Ronald headed over to try to stop him."

Every jolt and turn was agonizing and I hissed with pain as we stopped short for a traffic light. Hank noticed and his eyes flared with anger as he asked, "Joe's doing?"

I nodded and asked, "What made you attack Nasty Joe? You're scared of your own shadow. What got into you?"

Hank rolled his eyes again as he spoke. "Soon as he saw me and Ronald he started threatening Ronald. Said if he didn't hand me over he'd knock his teeth in. I was scared for my new master and scared of going back to Joe's. They started shoving and something in me just snapped. People thought I had rabies . . . I just went mad!"

"Thanks, big fellow," croaked Ugly Ben. "You helped save my buddy's life."

Hank glanced sadly at me. Ugly Ben could see what he was thinking.

"Hey, it's okay, my days were numbered anyway. Its better'n freezing to death come winter. And it sure beats getting your brains blown out in the garbage dump. Doc Jones explained how they do it – it's a peaceful way of going."

Hank's sorrowful eyes rested mournfully on Ugly Ben for the remainder of the journey and I was too heartsick to say another word. Ugly Ben put his head down on his paws, closed his eyes, and pretended to nap.

Chapter Fourteen

Hank and Ugly Ben were whisked off by uniformed attendants while I was carried gently into a hospital room and placed on an examining table that reeked of disinfectant. I hissed repeatedly as the doctor's hands prodded and explored. Dora, his assistant, helped hold me during the examination.

Dora massaged behind my ears, then scratched beneath my chin. She smiled reassuringly as she said to me, "You'll be just fine, puss, not to worry." I replied with a weak, un-Siamese-like meow, then lay down my head.

"Nothing broken, but he's badly bruised. Be a while before he resumes normal mobility," said the doctor.

After I was given an injection I was taken to a small room full of clean pens. There seemed to be hundreds of rooms filled with thousands of noisy cats and dogs. I learned later that there were three hundred dogs and cats in the building. By the time they settled me in my cage I was so groggy from my shot I hardly took notice of the stir my arrival caused among the other animals. I dragged my body as far to the back of my metal cage as I could and quickly fell into a deep, exhausted slumber.

The morning breakfast activities, accompanied by the excited barking of dogs and meowing cats, awakened me. Two of the attendants cleaned and disinfected the cages, replacing the newspaper flooring and litter boxes with a fresh supply. I sniffed the air as the attendants opened blue labeled tins of cat food and filled little metal basins from the large trolley. Similar basins were filled with water.

The workers stopped occasionally to chat with or stroke a friendly cat or dog. They moved up the row of cages with their trolley, commenting on the new arrivals.

"Is this the dog that attacked someone last night?" asked the older attendant. "He sure doesn't look like the unfriendly type." As they stood curiously in front of a cage across from me to my right, I realized it was occupied by Hank.

Although I stared hard at the cage I could only see his paws and part of his head because Hank was huddled right up against the wall. I could easily imagine the frightened pleading eyes looking up at the two attendants. One commented, "Poor wretch – look at him. Scared out of his wits. Let's have a look at his cat friend next door."

Ugly Ben looked through the bars of his cage. He gazed lazily at the workers, then closed his eyes. Ignoring his food, he went back to sleep.

"Sure is a battered old tom. There won't be anyone coming around to claim that poor old soul," remarked the younger attendant.

Some animals responded with hostility or cowered in fear but most of them, especially a big black dog, clamored for affection when their turn came to be fed. I stared cautiously at the women when it was my turn to be fed and hissed a warning when one tried to stroke me.

One attendant stopped and looked lovingly around the room at all of us as though she wished she could take us home. She smiled and reminded her assistant, "Don't forget we're supposed to keep an eye out for the cat that's been reported missing by the Fifty-First Division."

"Oh yeah," she replied, "the cop's cat, Ringer. Imagine the cops putting out a missing feline report."

"They say he was the best mouser they ever had. Apparently the cat was extremely friendly. They really want him back badly."

Eventually the noisy animals settled down to their meals and after-breakfast grooming. I was able to relax somewhat. I tried standing up but it was a painful business. I sank to the floor again. Grooming was a tedious affair as well since I could hardly lift or move my hind legs. I was grateful that at least I could move them. I called over to Hank, "How long do you think they'll keep us here, Hank?"

"Your guess is as good as mine," he responded. "By the way, there's something I forgot to tell you."

My ears perked forward as he continued. "Cindy's owners took her out for a stroll before dinner last evening and she led them straight to my place."

"Did Mark and Helen meet your new owner?"

"Sure did. Ronald told them all about Joe and now the Armstrongs are really riled!"

"Hear that, Ugly Ben?" I called.

"That you, Shalom?" he croaked.

"Yeah, pal." I repeated the news Hank had just given me.

He replied, "Well, whad'ya know. The streets of Rosedale will soon be safe to walk again."

"Lucky bums," grumbled a thin tortoise shell cat. "We're constantly hassled by people in the downtown section. I should have moved north long ago."

This opened up conversation among the animals that went on for some time before we were interrupted with the arrival of a newcomer. Hank greeted the cat with a surprised yelp and exclaimed, "It's Subway Pete!"

Ugly Ben, Hank and I pressed our noses through the bars and strained for a glimpse of Subway Pete. His body lay still and lifeless over the attendant's arm. I scented a strong medicinal odor as he was eased carefully to the floor of a cage near Ugly Ben. I stared in disbelief at his bandaged tail and unconscious form. The place became a circus again with animals barking or meowing, scratching and moving restlessly about their cages. The black dog thumped his tail noisily against the back of his metal cage and started howling for some unexplained reason. This set off a frenzied barking in other rooms, upsetting the more nervous cats who joined the noisy hue and cry.

"Shut up, the whole lot of you!" snarled an angry gray feline. "This place is an absolute madhouse! Just shut up, why don't ya?"

Because Subway Pete lay absolutely still, I knew it was no use calling out to him. I fastened my gaze unwaveringly on him for a long time, oblivious to all that went on around me. Later, two workers arrived to serve a midday snack. I stared intently as they stopped to examine Subway Pete.

"Is this the one?" asked the younger person.

"Sure looks like it."

"Okay. I'll phone right away for one of them to come in and identify him. Doc says there's a news reporter that wants to drop over and cover the story if he turns out to be the one."

I wished Subway Pete would wake from his anesthetic stupor and tell us what on earth was happening!

"What's going on?" inquired Ugly Ben.

"What's this about a news reporter?" asked a curious orange cat. "Anyone here know that cat? He famous or something?"

"Yeah, what's going on?" asked a German Shepherd pup.

The animals started talking excitedly and everyone had a theory about the mysterious newcomer.

"It's got to be mistaken identity," grumbled Ugly Ben. "I've known the kid for years. He never did a newsworthy thing in his life."

"Yeah, but look at his tail—obviously something unusual happened to him," said the black dog.

Another cat suggested he'd had some kind of unique accident. "Lots o' times you hear stories about cats that survive house fires or falls from tall buildings. I sure wish that dude would wake up! I'm dying from curiosity."

Subway Pete was still sleeping half an hour later when the doctor brought a police officer in to look him over. The officer removed his hat and stood scratching thoughtfully at his head.

"He sure looks like our missing Ringer. Same markings . . . white feet . . . heart-shaped white spot on his chest. Hmmm. Even the ears . . . black with that white patch on his forehead. Markings on the back though . . . seems our cat had more white markings . . . but then I could be wrong. Man, it's hard to say for sure."

The doctor laughed. "Now you know how people feel when they have to identify someone in a lineup."

"Yeah," replied the officer with a grin. "It's not easy. But this is weird. If this isn't our guy, this fellow's practically his twin. What happened to his tail?"

"Oh, that. Sad thing. It looked like someone took a knife or hatchet to him. Had to amputate a good part of the tail. May have been an accident but it beats me what caused it. Couldn't have been a car or slammed door."

The officer studied Subway Pete closely, then said, "He may not be our mouser but he sure looks like him. Our own Ringer's been missing quite a long time now so I reckon we may as well adopt this little look-alike. Give us a call when he's on his feet and ready to start work. He's got a cushy job as 'Pest Control Officer' waiting for him down at Fifty-First Precinct."

The doctor smiled and said, "There's a news reporter that wants to write this up as a feature article. He'll be over for photos when puss wakes up. Okay if he drops by for an interview at Fifty-First?"

"Sounds great! Send him over." The officer stopped to pet the black dog's nose through the bars as he left the room.

Subway Pete woke up for a few minutes during the supper feeding but was too groggy to understand much of what we said. The only thing that really registered in his mind was that we had escaped Nasty Joe.

"Glad you're all safe," he mumbled happily as he drifted off to sleep again.

"But Subway Pete," I called happily, "you're famous! You have a home and an exciting new job! Your picture's gonna be on all the newsstands! Wow, that's as exciting as winning Grand Champion!"

"S'nice," he mumbled groggily. "S'nice you gotta job. I gotta sleep. . .tired. . .mrrrff."

"But Subway. . . ."

"Forget it," Hank advised. "He's totally out of it. Wait'll he's bright-eyed and bushy-tailed again."

When Subway Pete was alert and done eating, everyone tried to tell him at once what was happening.

"But . . . but I never even heard of the Fifty-First Precinct. I'm not their cat. . . ."

"It doesn't matter, fellow," said Ugly Ben. "You're almost a carbon copy of the cat they lost so they're taking you anyway."

"Lucky bum," said the tortoise shell cat.

"Owrowrrrr!" crowed Subway Pete. "Pest Control Officer – wow! They won't be disappointed, fellows, I'm a killer-diller mouser!"

"Subway Pete – what on earth happened to your tail?" I asked.

"Oh that," he said sheepishly. "I'd rather not say."

Naturally this started the whole room full of animals clamoring again as they begged him to tell.

"Hmph. Very stupid of me, but I was in an awful state . . . thought Nasty Joe was after me. I was heading across the ravine . . . running for my life, man and suddenly this subway train comes barreling down the tracks. I panicked! I knew it was too close but I thought I'd try for it anyway. Well, most of me made it as you can see."

This got a good laugh out of everyone, even the crabby gray.

"Now if you ladies and gentlemen will excuse me, I must groom myself for that photographer."

I sighed happily as he sat cleaning his fur. He looked over at me once and winked, grinning the old lopsided grin. I looked at Hank who was dozing contentedly, then I looked at Ugly Ben.

He was wheezing, half-asleep and smiling happily. I sighed again, but with sadness. He really was at peace, but this did not comfort me much. I would miss him. All of us would miss him. Our courageous friend had lived his life to the full in spite of hardship and suffering and now faced death with dignity.

Subway Pete returned from his photography session in the office, grinning like a true celebrity.

"It's a dream," he proclaimed as he stretched out on the cage floor. "I can't believe this is happening to me. It's going to be in the weekend edition – day after tomorrow."

"Maybe your story will inspire more people to take in strays," said the orange cat.

"Hey, yeah. This could be good news for us too," said the black dog as he thumped his tail noisily against the metal cage wall.

Chapter Fifteen

Our first visitors the following day were the Armstrongs and Ronald. Helen cried out eagerly to her husband, "Oh Mark, I wish we could take all of them home."

Ronald leaned down to speak to Hank and grinned as the dog licked at his fingers through the slender iron bars. Then he said, "You're comin' home with me, old boy. Joe ain't gonna bother you ever again. Me and the Armstrongs are gonna put that cat-hating drug dealer out of circulation for a while. I can't wait to see his face in court."

Hank just rolled his eyes and gazed up lovingly at Ronald.

"Mark," declared Helen firmly, "we must take one of them home. How can you resist?"

Her husband replied laughingly, "We already have six dogs and two cats."

"One more! What's one more cat, please?"

"Well. . . ."

"Oh thank you!" she exclaimed, clasping her hands and gazing around. Instead of looking us over she turned to the attendant and asked, "Which cat has the least chance of being adopted?"

"You serious?" asked the young man.

"Absolutely."

He looked at Mark who shrugged good-naturedly. "She's the boss," joked Mark.

The worker smiled and walked straight to Ugly Ben's cage. "You sure, lady? He's old and he's sick. This ugly fellow's going to cost you a pretty penny in vet's fees."

The indignant Ugly Ben lifted his old head and stared at the worker so fiercely that he hesitated to open the cage.

Helen made him open the gate and as she scratched the asthmatic cat under the chin, she looked into Ugly Ben's golden eyes and said to her husband, "He's a grand old gentleman. Ugly – but grand. And he's got character galore. Can't you picture this old grandad curled in front of the fireplace on cold wintry nights, darling? Oh my – he'll love that!"

"Yeah, guess so."

"My next book is going to be about an old, old stray cat who's led a long and exciting life and sits abandoned in the Humane Society's Animal Shelter, looking sadly into the eyes of each. . . ."

"This is not the time to wax eloquent about your next novel. If he sparks your creative genius you're welcome to him."

Helen hugged her husband and then gathered Ugly Ben up in her arms. Ugly Ben's guttural purr amused her and she teased, "He sounds like he's choking on a bone or something."

"Yeah? It's me that's going to be all choked up when the vet bills start rolling in."

Ugly Ben croaked his happy farewell as the Armstrongs, together with Ronald and Hank, walked toward the exit. Other animals joined in as we called out goodbyes, congratulating Ugly Ben and wishing him luck. Hank turned in the doorway and barked an excited farewell as the door closed quietly behind them. I peeked over at Subway Pete who commented eagerly, "Well, little buddy—you'll probably be the next to go. I reckon Wilkes will be here right after work. How're the old hind legs?"

"Somewhat better today. I guess I'll be a while recovering. And how's the old tail?"

"Pickin' sore! They really stitched up the old stump good!"

"You're gonna be cute as a half-tailed cat."

"Aw shuddup!"

"Rowowrrrr, he's a touchy one," I teased.

That afternoon brought still another great surprise. I was awakened from sleep by a worker who announced, "This is the Siamese, but there must be some mistake, folks. Fellow by the name of Wilkes is picking him up tonight. Claims it's his cat."

Even before I opened my eyes, I knew by their scent it was the Penners! I scented my mother's odor on them as well and would have leaped up for joy were it not for my crippled hind legs. As it was, I could only hobble to the gate where I flopped over on my side, purring loud enough to be heard a block away. I yowled raucously until the gate was unlatched and my owners were able to stroke and scratch me in the familiar way I'd missed so much.

"Oh mercy, Shalom, look at your face—and that poor ear," cried Mrs. Penner. "I shall never forgive myself for letting you escape."

"It wasn't your fault, dear. We really don't know how it happened," Mr. Penner comforted.

"Yes, yes, I know," she said as she cuddled me carefully in her arms. "But I still blame myself. Oh poor sweetheart. You're coming home with me right this minute."

The worker sputtered nervously, "Uh, I'm sorry, madam, sir, but there's another gentleman. . . ."

"Yes, well, that other gentleman may jump in the lake. Look at this cat! Is this how he takes care of his animals? This happens to be Grand Champion stock."

"I'm sure there's some kind of explanation. Perhaps you're mistaken? Siamese do look very much alike. . . ."

"Ordinary Siamese perhaps, young man, but Grand Champion caliber like this are one in ten thousand. I would know this cat anywhere. He's ours and we're taking him home immediately. We've gone to a great deal of trouble trying to locate this cat and we're not about to. . . ."

"Now calm down, dear," Mr. Penner interrupted politely. "I'm sure this can all be sorted out with a few phone calls. May I use your phone? Do you have the other gentleman's number?"

The worker looked relieved and hurried out with Mr. Penner to the phone. A smiling Mrs. Penner insisted on waiting with me as she declared, "I'm not letting this dear cat out of my arms for one second!"

"I say, old buddy," joked Subway Pete, "what was all that talk about them not wanting you anymore now that you're all washed up as a show cat?"

"I'm so happy," I purred. "My only regret is. . . ."

"Yeah?"

"I'll miss Simcha and Angie."

"That's a bit of a shame."

"And I'll miss you too."

"Same here, little buddy. I can't believe it's been less than a week since you wandered into the park like a scared little kitten."

Mrs. Penner kissed me repeatedly and buried her nose in my fur while I purred ecstatically. Mr. Penner appeared at the door and I could see by the smile on his face that I would be going home with them. "Okay Lorna," he announced, "we can take our baby home. Believe it or not, that Wilkes fellow's the one whose Siamese took Grand Champion this year."

"That's amazing! But how on earth did. . . ."

Mr. Penner held his hand up laughing and told her it was a long story. "Our Shalom has had quite a few adventures. Let's head home and I'll tell you everything on the way."

I strained for one last glance at Subway Pete as we made our way to the door. He grinned happily as we passed his cage. "So long kid. I'll miss ya!"

"Goodbye, Subway Pete," I cried as the door began to close behind us. "Goodbye! Goodbye!"

Chapter Sixteen

Mother and I spent many hours sunning in our favorite window sill, discussing the adventures I'd had. She could not seem to get enough of grooming me those first few days and I enjoyed being fussed over like a kitten again. One day I told her about Angie and Simcha and wondered sadly if I would ever see them again.

Later that day, as I lay curled up on the sofa, I overheard the Penners discussing me. Mr. Penner surprised me greatly by announcing, "That Wilkes fellow phoned again."

"He did?"

"Upped his bid again. He really wants Shalom. Says his kid is badgering him constantly—she's even offering to donate some of her own money. He says that Mrs. Wilkes thinks our Shalom and their Simcha would make an ideal couple!"

"Hmmm."

I sat up quivering with elation and meowed loudly. That amused them. Mrs. Penner laughed as she commented, "You'd almost think he understands. Do you think he would object if we sold him to the Wilkes?"

I responded with my fullest top-volume Siamese yowl so they could not possibly fail to understand my desire. "Yes indeed. I would love to be sold to the Wilkes," I meowed anxiously. Never in my life had I so wished I could speak like a human! I dare say, they must have understood me, for the following evening Mr. Wilkes and Angie stood at our door, smiling broadly, with a Simcha-scented carrying cage in their hands. Mother was so thrilled she meowed and ran excitedly back and forth across the room. She hurried over to Angie and rubbed against her ankles, then sat demurely watching as I was placed inside the carrier. While the Penners visited with Mr. Wilkes and Angie, Mother came and sat in front of the cage. She smiled serenely, her beautiful eyes aglow. "Your father and I. . ." she began, then hesitated.

"Yes?" I coaxed.

"It was an arranged marriage too," she stated shyly.

"And?" I teased.

"Well, it was love at first sight. I'm sure you'll be very, very happy."

I did not need to reply. My smile said it all!

If only Subway Pete could have seen the look on Big Tom's face the first time Simcha and I took our evening walk with Angie. There was no mistaking my new status in the Wilkes's household. We had matching leashes with shimmering jewel-studded collars. As we strolled down the block, we had eyes only for each other. Big Tom sat on the opposite side of the road under the streetlight, staring in amazement. For once he had nothing to say and as we passed by, Simcha and I stopped, arched our backs and hissed furiously at him. He was up the street and around the corner in no time at all. It didn't take long for word to get around about what he had done to Subway Pete and me, and last I heard, he'd been run out of Rosedale by Hank and Cindy and several of their dog buddies.

"It's not fair," I complained to Simcha as we sauntered along the walk. "You'll be off to all kinds of competitions and modeling assignments and glamorous movie productions - things we could have done together, but now Big Tom has ruined all that."

"Shalom, my darling – I will not listen to your self-pity," she replied firmly. "You may never be Grand Champion in the public eye but you're my Grand Champion and you're a hero as well. When I realized you'd stayed and fought for your best friend, knowing it could cost you your career, maybe even your life, why I just . . . I. . ." she smiled shyly and concluded, "Well – how could I help but love you?"

"But . . . but you never showed it. I thought. . . ."

"Oh silly!" she laughed delicately. "You knew I wasn't free to marry the cat of my choice. You knew my marriage would be planned and arranged by the Wilkes. It would have been cruel to tell you how I felt."

"Oh yes, yes, you're quite right," I replied. "It's a marvel how wonderfully everything has worked out for us. I doubt there's a happier cat in all Rosedale."

"Oh, I'm so glad that you feel that way too," replied Simcha. "We mustn't allow Big Tom's wickedness to spoil our happiness."

"Not only are you beautiful," I replied, "you're also wise. I shall not allow my disappointments to keep me from enjoying all these good things."

Simcha purred and leaned her head happily on my shoulder, causing Angie to chuckle fondly. "Oh, what darlings you are. You must promise to start a family as soon as possible. I want lots and lots of kittens to adore and fuss over. Mum says your names will soon become a legend among international cat breeders. And I bet your beautiful kittens will all be Grand Champions – every one of them – and people will . . . ."

"Oh my goodness, listen to her," exclaimed Simcha.

"Well – she always did want cats by the dozens," I teased. "Maybe she'll get her wish now."

During the summer months we were visited by our old friends, sometimes during our evening walks or out by the big kitchen window. One evening we were delighted to see Ugly Ben hobbling across the lawn. He grunted happily as we greeted him. He made his way carefully onto the spacious window ledge and settled contentedly. My friend had filled out considerably. I was pleased to see how shiny and healthy his fur looked. There was still a slight asthmatic wheeze but I could see he was much more energetic.

"It's a great life over there," he said, referring to his new home. "Never had it so good. How's them legs of yours, sonny?"

"Much better," I replied. "There's still a bit of stiffness but I get around fine."

"And the little lady?"

"Oh I'm fine, Ugly Ben. We're glad to see you looking so well," Simcha responded affectionately.

"Yup. That wedding of yours is still the talk of the whole Rosedale cat community. Wish Subway Pete coulda known."

"I sure do miss the guy," I replied.

Ugly Ben chuckled mischievously. "He'd a' hooted like a hyena about them dogs running Big Tom outta the neighborhood. Cindy and the pups send their love, 'cept they ain't pups no more. They'll soon be adopted. Hank sends fond regards too. Him and Ronald come over fairly regular. Those two are mighty fond of the Armstrongs. They've been real kind to him and his dog. In fact, Ronald's got himself a job now and he don't look so scruffy no more. Even old Hank is losing his hangdog look."

We laughed at this and Ugly Ben shifted into a sitting position. He scratched leisurely behind one ear and grinned. "See that? It's been a dog's age since I was able to get at them fleas with a hind leg. I'm feelin' better'n I've felt in years."

"I have never had a flea," said Simcha primly.

Ugly Ben stopped his leg in midair and stared at Simcha, then looked at me. "She serious?" he asked.

"Yup."

"Weird eh?"

"Yup."

"Imagine that," he mumbled as he settled again on the ledge. "Never had a flea bite in her whole life. Hmmm."

"How are things going with Doc Jones and Pretty Sal?" I asked.

"You heard about the youngsters, I reckon. Those little fellows are quite something. Three of them are pure white like their ma and the fourth one looks like Doc Jones. You'll never guess the latest though, I bet. You heard yet?" Ugly Ben smiled happily. We pricked our ears forward eagerly, as he announced "Pretty Sal's been adopted – her and the four little ones!"

"Oh how fabulous!" cried Simcha. "How. . . where. . . ?"

"It was super," said Ugly Ben. "Happened the night Doc Jones took her and the kids along on his hospital rounds. He told me the vet went wild over Sal and the kids and adopted them on the spot. Kids are sure to find good homes now."

All of us sighed happily.

As we continued gossiping about our friends, Simcha listened in amusement. Ugly Ben informed me scornfully, "Rumor has it that Miss Calico has taken a shine to Preacher Ted but he's not letting on if the feeling is mutual."

"I don't think she's his type anyway," I said. "She seems to prefer the stray lifestyle."

"You get the odd one like that," he replied. "Truckin' Sam's the same way. Doesn't want to be tied down to people. But most strays are desperate to find a home."

We sat in silence. I thought of cats like Timid Gray who needed human love and care but would probably never be adopted because of her fear of people. Conversation eventually got around to Subway Pete, and Simcha told Ugly Ben about the news clipping about Subway Pete that Angie had pasted into her scrapbook.

"The news article has a charming photo of Subway Pete perched on top of a policeman's hat with a subtitle that reads, 'SHE'S THE CAT'S MEOW.'"

"She?" interrupted Ugly Ben.

"Yeah," I replied. "I nearly fell off Angie's lap laughing when I noticed they referred to my buddy as 'she,' but that'll keep him humble."

We chuckled together and Simcha continued. "The article said that the police at Fifty-First Division in Regent Park have enlisted him as police constable in charge of mouse patrol. I don't think Subway Pete likes his new name though. They call him 'Stubby' because of his missing tail."

"Oh well," grunted Ugly Ben, "that'll keep him humble too."

"The police figured some 'low life' hacked off his tail with a hacksaw," I said. "I guess that's one case they'll never solve."

"What else does the paper say? he asked eagerly.

Simcha replied, "The Toronto Sun article says that the police filed a missing feline report and conducted an all-out cat hunt but neither hair nor tail of Constable Ringer was ever seen again. The police called him Ringer because of the ring at the end of the tail and that ring was the all-important missing clue on Subway Pete! Other than that they said he was "almost a ringer for Ringer." "Totally incredible," mumbled Ugly Ben.

"Isn't it," I replied.

"So anyway," concluded Simcha, "he now has one of the most prestigious positions a cat could ever hope to attain. Imagine – he's a police constable now."

"Yup," said Uncle Ben proudly, "and I wouldn't be surprised if he makes it all the way up to mayor's assistant!"

"You just never know," said Simcha.

"You just never know," I echoed as I gazed up into the evening sky. Ugly Ben and Simcha looked up at the stars as well and we sat in companionable silence listening to night sounds and chirping crickets. The air was warm and fragrant and a beautiful full moon shone radiantly down. The whole world seemed at peace and I sighed contentedly. I thought again that I must truly be the happiest cat in all of Rosedale - perhaps even in all the world!

ABOUT THE AUTHOR

Gloria Guenther resides in Langley, British Columbia. Gloria and Harvey, her husband, have spent a number of years in mission ministries in England and Toronto, Canada. They now work in camp ministries in British Columbia. The Guenthers have three children.

Gloria is active in a variety of groups, including a writer's group. She continually seeks to express her desires and dreams through writing. Gloria loves to write, and also loves cats. This book has grown out of her love for and interest in cats. Not only has she observed cats first hand, being the happy owner of four, but she has shown tremendous talent in portraying them in various poses. Gloria is able to combine her writing skills with excellent artistic talent.